Praise f
The Lazy Ger

"With wisdom, humor, and practicality, Kendra Adachi gives us a system to get stuff done without losing ourselves in the process. Not only will this book reengineer how you approach life, but you will come away feeling more yourself. And nothing is more powerful than living a life of purpose and accomplishment while at the same time feeling more yourself than ever before."

—BRI MCKOY, author of *Come & Eat*

"In a world that is constantly screaming to do more and do it perfectly, *The Lazy Genius Way* rushes to the rescue. Kendra gently takes us by the hand and helps us know that we don't have to be the best at everything. We can actually learn to enjoy the things we love and even happily thrive while doing the things we don't love."

—JESSICA THOMPSON, national speaker and coauthor of *Give Them Grace*

"Reading this approachable, practical book will feel like spending an afternoon with a wise and cool big sister who is helping you get your life together. Without an ounce of shame or guilt, Kendra gives you permission to care about the things that really matter to you and to be lazy about the things that don't. I only wish I could have read this book twenty years ago."

—SARAH BESSEY, author of *Miracles and Other Reasonable Things*

"Kendra has a heart for infusing the mundane and practical with a profound sacredness. Frankly, it's infuriating how she manages to be effortlessly instructional, inspirational, and hilarious all at the same time, but the world is such a better place for it. I've never been more thankful for someone's voice."

—KNOX MCCOY, author of *All Things Reconsidered*

"If you've been taught that nothing good comes from being lazy, get ready to let Kendra change your mind and life forever. Spoiler: laziness is *the* powerful tool that frees you to be a genius where it really matters. I wish I had this eye-opening book twenty years ago."

—MYQUILLYN SMITH, *Wall Street Journal* bestselling author of *Cozy Minimalist Home*

"*The Lazy Genius Way* is a recipe for creating a generous, less stressed domestic life. Kendra's suggestions for thoughtful routines in place of rigid rules will leave the reader feeling settled and prepared for the changing rhythms of both family life and personal growth. Also, she is what experts refer to as a hoot."

—GINA SMITH and S. D. SMITH, author of The Green Ember series

"*The Lazy Genius Way* is the guidebook for adulting that we've been waiting for, and Kendra Adachi—with the kind practicality of Leslie Knope, the fierceness of Beyoncé, and the charms of Hermione—is the leader we'll love forever. Boiled down to what matters most, daily life suddenly seems more manageable. Delivered with Kendra's classic blend of wit and wisdom, it even seems more fun."

—SHANNAN MARTIN, author of *The Ministry of Ordinary Places* and *Falling Free*

"As a longtime fan of *The Lazy Genius Podcast,* I could not be more excited about this book. Kendra has a gift for asking questions that helps you prioritize the parts of your life that really matter and let go of the parts that don't. She doesn't preach or pressure; she inquires and encourages. As she admits, it's not easy to manage the seemingly constant demands of running a house, planning meals, hosting relatives, and creating and maintaining holiday traditions, all while finding time for your own work and self-care. But Kendra makes it all a lot easier!"

—JENNA FISCHER, actor, author of *The Actor's Life,* and cohost of the *Office Ladies* podcast

"Fun and funny, warm and wise: figuring out how to get your life together has never been so entertaining."

—ANNE BOGEL, author of *Don't Overthink It* and creator of the *Modern Mrs. Darcy* blog

"*The Lazy Genius Way* has made me rethink all my current systems in the best way possible. I am more clearheaded while making decisions after reading this book."

—LAURA TREMAINE, host of the *10 Things to Tell You* podcast

"I've known Kendra for several years now, and I don't think I've met anyone else who embodies both a kindhearted, fun-to-be-around spirit and the practicality of a go-to friend who knows how to get things done. When you need a friend to boss you around in only the *best* way possible, pick up this book and let Kendra do it. Her wisdom about a range of topics, from making friends to cleaning the kitchen, will light a fire under you so you can do what matters and chill about the rest."

—TSH OXENREIDER, author of *At Home in the World* and *Shadow & Light*

"I always followed the lazy path when it came to my home. The results of that approach were not surprising—trash bins stuffed with take-out boxes, moldy laundry in the washer, and so much chaos. But Kendra Adachi offers a better way. The Lazy Genius Way doesn't mean you have to become a gourmet chef or start cleaning the baseboards with a toothbrush. Kendra will meet you in the middle. She offers easy steps that will have you marking off your list in record time without sacrificing every free moment you have. Kendra helps us make space for tasks and television. She finds time for us to solve problems and scroll Instagram. The Lazy Genius Way is the perfect way."

—JAMIE GOLDEN, cohost of *The Popcast with Knox and Jamie*

THE LAZY GENIUS WAY

EMBRACE WHAT MATTERS, DITCH WHAT DOESN'T, AND GET STUFF DONE

KENDRA ADACHI

WATERBROOK

Published in the United States by WaterBrook, an imprint of
Random House, a division of Penguin Random House LLC.

WATERBROOK® and its deer colophon are
registered trademarks of Penguin Random House LLC.

The author is represented by Alive Literary Agency, www.aliveliterary.com.

This work contains an excerpt from the forthcoming work *The PLAN* by
Kendra Adachi. This excerpt has been set for this edition only and may not
reflect the final content of the forthcoming edition.

Paperback ISBN 978-0-525-65393-6

The Library of Congress has cataloged the hardcover edition as follows:
Names: Adachi, Kendra, author.
Title: The lazy genius way : embrace what matters, ditch what doesn't,
and get stuff done / Kendra Adachi.
Description: First edition. | Colorado Springs : WaterBrook, 2020. |
Includes bibliographical references.
Identifiers: LCCN 2019046948 | ISBN 9780525653912 (hardcover) |
ISBN 9780525653929 (ebook)
Subjects: LCSH: Simplicity. | Thought and thinking.
Classification: LCC BJ1496 .A33 2020 | DDC 158.1—dc23
LC record available at https://lccn.loc.gov/2019046948

Printed in the United States of America on acid-free paper

waterbrookmultnomah.com

8 9 7

Trade Paperback Edition

SPECIAL SALES
Most WaterBrook books are available at special quantity discounts when
purchased in bulk by corporations, organizations, and special-interest groups.
Custom imprinting or excerpting can also be done to fit special needs. For
information, please email specialmarketscms@penguinrandomhouse.com.

FOREWORD

Some moments—such as weddings, births, graduations, and proposals—carve a deep groove in our memories because they mark our lives in a significant way. Other moments remain embedded in time because they hold hands with deep emotions like joy, shock, passion, or grief. Still, life is mostly made up of the kinds of moments that may seem ordinary while you live them but are the ones you return to in gratitude. It's not because they were necessarily remarkable but because they shaped the contours of your life one small moment at a time.

In the spring of 2008, my husband, John, and I were in the middle of packing up all our worldly belongings to move to a house across town. In addition to the regular stress that accompanies moving, John was about a year into a new job at a local church, and we had three children ages four and under. It seemed every area of our life was touched by either chaos or transition, and I was weeks past ready for both to be over.

A few days before the closing, all our furniture was at the new house, but we still had some last-minute items we needed to pack up in the old one: condiments in the fridge, stacks of junk mail on the counter, plastic bins with no lids in the dining room, and a few final kitchen drawers filled with misfit office supplies, tangled wires, and unidentifiable gadget leftovers. As it turns out, you don't just get to move with the stuff you like. You have to move with *everything*. I was ready to set the remaining items on fire so we didn't have to pack or unpack them. But instead of lighting a match, I called a friend.

While John stayed with our kids at the new house, my friend came to help me empty the old house of those few straggling possessions and load my car one last time. If you've been alive for five minutes, maybe you already know this was a fairly vulnerable ask. I had known this friend for only about a year at this point, and I was shy about asking her over for dinner—much less inviting her to help me transport the dregs of our life from our old house to our new one. She would see my obvious disorganization and the unnecessary junk I held on to. Moreover, she would see me in all my frazzled, unshowered, end-of-my-rope glory.

Still, she came. We worked together in silence, carrying lidless plastic containers filled with random tools, freezer items, and lightbulbs out to the yard to load into our cars. I remember feeling relief that she didn't wait for my direction (which honestly at that point would have probably been to point to the yard and hand her a match). Instead, she saw what needed doing, and she worked quickly, without commentary, helping me finish up the last embarrassing loads and get the job done. What I remember most about that day was her kind silence and her present posture.

If you haven't figured it out yet, that friend was Kendra Adachi. And though that move was more than ten years ago, though that afternoon was not accompanied by a single meaningful conversation or a traditionally significant moment, the memory revisits me often, and I tear up thinking of it even now. Because instead of approaching that move like a Lazy Genius, I handled it more like an overworked fool. I did the wrong things in the wrong order, feeling shame for the state of my house and the chaos in my life.

Meanwhile, Kendra is an expert at creating systems to finish tasks. She is a master at doing the right things in the right order for the right reasons, from packing a box to hosting a party. While it was, of course, a gift to have a friend willing to help me move—and to be able to trust a friend to see me at my frantic worst—the reason this memory stands out for me goes even deeper than that. It stands out because the thing I felt I was failing so miserably at was the very thing she was so *good* at, and still she showed up for me, filled with compassion, miles from judgment. She showed up for me in love.

The book you now hold is evidence of that love. You may have picked it up because you need help getting stuff done. She will certainly help you do that. But efficient systems fail to deliver if they're implemented without kindness. That's the unique gift of this book and why I'm so grateful to Kendra for finally writing it down.

The reason *The Lazy Genius Way* has the potential to change how you live your life is not simply because of its practical tips but because of the spirit in which they are offered. From the way you clean your kitchen to the way you start your day, being a Lazy Genius is not about doing things the *right* way but about finally finding *your own* way. You won't hear empty mantras shaming you into doing things better. Instead, you'll be encouraged to decide what matters for you, and you'll receive permission to gently leave the rest behind.

It's been ten years since my family moved. Since then, Kendra and I have shared countless moments together, and I no longer feel any shadow of embarrassment when she sees me at my rock-bottom worst. This transformation started the day she showed up ready to help me, even though she could have bossed me into ways of doing it better. But she didn't shame me then, and she won't shame you either. Kendra is teaching me to be a genius about the things that matter and lazy about the things that don't. Before you give up on yourself and allow chaos to tempt you to burn the house down, back away from the matches and read this kind, life-giving, practical book.

—Emily P. Freeman
author of *The Next Right Thing*

CONTENTS

THE LAZY GENIUS WAY

INTRODUCTION

(Please Don't Skip It)

I'm not a mom who plays. I mean, I will, but I personally don't like knocking down a stack of blocks twenty thousand times in a row, no matter how much joy it brings my kids.*

Thankfully, my husband is a dad who plays. A few summers ago, he came up big while we were vacationing at the beach. He dug an impressive hole in the sand, a hole so deep you had to lean over the edge to see the bottom. Then, with the enthusiasm of a carnival showman, he got all three kids to race back and forth from the ocean, carrying buckets of water to fill the hole as quickly as they could.

Over and over again, they hauled and poured, hauled and poured.

But that hole would not fill up.

Every single drop soaked back into the sand, taunting them in their efforts. Because my kids are adorable little weirdos, they thought it was fun and played the game for a long while—that is, until a flock of aggressive seagulls became more interesting.

---

*I have three, by the way. Sam is in fourth grade and obsessed with *Minecraft,* Ben is in second grade and obsessed with painting the *Mona Lisa,* and Annie is in preschool and obsessed with me.

As they ran off to chase the birds, I saw the discarded buckets surrounding the empty hole and realized I was looking at a metaphor of my life. Maybe it's one for yours too.

Here's what we do as women.* We pick our spot in the sand to dig a hole, checking to see if the women around us are choosing similar (or, gulp, *better*) spots, trying not to be distracted by their motherly patience and bikini bodies. We start digging, hoping the hole is deep enough and headed in the right direction. Where is it going? No idea, but who cares. Everyone else is digging, so we dig too.

Eventually it's time to start hauling buckets to fill the hole. We carry load after load of "water"—color-coded calendars, room-mom responsibilities, meal plans, and work-life balance. We haul. We try. We sweat. And we watch that hole stay empty.

Now we're confused.

Does everyone else have this figured out? Is my hole too deep? And where is all the water going?

We pause to catch our breath, wondering if everyone else feels like an epic failure too. One person can't possibly keep up with a clean house, a fulfilling job, a well-adjusted family, an active social life, and a running regimen of fifteen miles a week, right?

With silence our only answer, we decide, *No, it's just me. I need to get it together.* What follows is a flurry of habit trackers, calendar overhauls, and internet rabbit holes to figure out how to be better, until we pass out from emotional exhaustion

---

*If you're a dude, please let this inform your understanding of how women are often wired and the pressures we feel due to the culture we're a part of. Also, thank you for reading this book even though I will unashamedly always use female pronouns.

or actual adrenal fatigue or we give up completely and head back to the beach house for a shame-filled margarita.

Cheers?

THE REAL REASON YOU'RE TIRED

You're not tired because laundry takes up more space on your couch than humans do, no one in your house seems to care about your work deadline, or your kid's school lunch rule is "grapes must be quartered." The tasks are plentiful, but you know your to-do list isn't solely to blame.

You're "on" all the time, trying to be present with your people, managing the emotions of everyone around you, carrying the invisible needs of strangers in line at the post office, and figuring out how to meet your own needs with whatever you have left over—assuming you know what your needs are in the first place.

It's too much. Or maybe it feels like too much because you haven't read the right book, listened to the right podcast, or found the right system.

I know that feeling. I've spent an embarrassing number of hours searching for the right tools to make my life feel under control, and I have the abandoned stack of planners and highlighted self-help books to prove it. Unnecessary spoiler alert: they didn't help.

On one side, I felt like I had to create a carbon copy of the author's life, even though I dislike going to bed early and don't travel to twenty cities a year speaking at events.

On the other side? Follow your dreams, girl. Apparently, my to-do list isn't the problem; my small-time thinking is.

Still, I highlighted dozens of passages, trying to MacGyver

together some kind of plan that made sense for me. Maybe the right combination of life hacks and inspirational quotes would keep me from lying awake in the middle of the night with worry. Yet despite book after book, quote after quote, and plan after plan, I stayed tired. Maybe you're reading this book because you feel it too.

I have good news. You don't need a new list of things to do; *you need a new way to see.*

WHY SIMPLIFYING DOESN'T WORK

It's the most common solution to feeling overwhelmed: simplify. Do less, have less, get on Instagram less. Cut down on commitments, outsource, and say no. But also give back to the community, join a book club, and grow heirloom tomatoes. Make your own baby food, run an impressive side hustle, and go on a regular date night with your spouse if you expect your marriage to survive. How is that simple? In my experience, marriage, entrepreneurship, and gardening are all super complicated.

For Christians, the concept of a simple life can feel even more muddled. Jesus was homeless, had twelve friends, and depended on the kindness of others for a meal and a bed. His life focused on a singular goal, and everything else was straightforward. But a little further back in the Bible, we find the (very misunderstood) Proverbs 31 woman who gets up before the sun, sews bed linens for her family, plants vineyards, and has strong arms.

Will someone please tell me what I'm supposed to care about so I can just live my life?

And that's why simplification is anything but simple. No

single voice can tell us how to live. Even within the biblical message of "love God and love people" lie a million possibilities of how that could look practically.

We need a filter that allows us to craft a life focusing only on what matters to us, not on what everyone else says *should* matter.

My friend, welcome to the Lazy Genius Way.

HOW TO READ THIS BOOK

Here's your new mantra: be a genius about the things that matter and lazy about the things that don't . . . *to you.*

As life circumstances change, needs and priorities follow suit. This book is designed to be a helpful reference through all those transitions, giving you language and tools to make room for what matters.

Each chapter highlights a Lazy Genius principle, with ideas to implement it immediately. One principle on its own

> **Here's your new mantra: be a genius about the things that matter and lazy about the things that don't . . . *to you.***

will have a tangible impact, but as you apply each to your daily life, you'll see how the thirteen principles can harmoniously create personalized solutions to your problems and illuminate the ones that don't matter so much.

You can quickly scan these pages for concrete steps and helpful lists and, when you have time, read more deeply as you create space to become your truest self. I encourage you to grab this book whenever you hit a wall in your routine, when a transition is looming, or when you feel the weight of busyness.

You'll learn better ways to do laundry, finish projects, and get dinner on the table. Praise! But beyond the practical, you'll learn to embrace a life that offers space for success and struggle, energy and exhaustion, clean houses and crappy meals. It all counts because it's all yours.

> **You'll learn better ways to do laundry, finish projects, and get dinner on the table. Praise! But beyond the practical, you'll learn to embrace a life that offers space for success and struggle, energy and exhaustion, clean houses and crappy meals. It all counts because it's all yours.**

Whether you're home with tiny humans, pursuing the corner office, lonely, busy, or bored, this book will help you name what matters, ditch what doesn't, and Lazy Genius a life full of both productivity and peace.

Let's get started.

HOW TO THINK
LIKE A LAZY GENIUS

My first job out of college was at the church where I spent my high school years and where, a few months earlier, I had gotten married. Many of my coworkers had known me since before I could drive a car, but now I was a grown-up with a husband and a job description.

I was eager to prove I belonged.

Once a month we had a morning staff meeting, and coworkers would take turns providing breakfast for everyone. Most months had the usual fare of grocery store muffins and fruit salad, and I remember thinking, *I can do better than this*.

I eventually signed up for breakfast duty not out of kindness but because I wanted *my* breakfast to be the gold standard. Yes, I cringe with humiliation as I publicly share such hubris, but as a self-righteous perfectionist, I was obsessed with keeping score, avoiding failure, and being impressive. Comparison and judgment were par for the course.*

Most folks paired up to provide the meal, but no, ma'am, not me. I was going to do this entire shindig on my own. I fig-

---

* If I had been cool enough to go to parties as a teenager, I wouldn't have been fun at them anyway.

ured weak, unimpressive people ask for help. Outwardly confident, inwardly crumbling people go solo.

Obviously, perfection was my standard—and not for the food alone. Despite the fact that my husband and I had zero dollars, I splurged on a couple of platters from Pottery Barn so that the food I served would look beautiful. I bought a linen tablecloth; the plastic ones at church would make my new platters look bad. I purchased one of those glass drink dispensers you see in *Southern Living* because perfection doesn't serve beverages from plastic pitchers. Fresh flowers, fancy napkins—you get the idea.

For the menu, I thought back to a few weeks earlier when we had breakfast at a friend's house and the entire group was in a stupor over his stuffed french toast: gooey, golden, and a definite contender for best breakfast ever. It was the perfect choice.

But here's the kicker: I didn't know how to make stuffed french toast. I knew how to cook a decent spaghetti sauce and was in the early stages of a near-perfect chocolate chip cookie, but my culinary skills weren't exactly versatile. Maybe if I had followed a recipe things would have worked out differently.

Alas, at the time, I thought recipes were also for the weak. So I set out to make not one but two types of stuffed french toast for thirty people, without a single instruction.

In case you don't know how stuffed french toast is made, let me quickly explain. You essentially make a sandwich, using a rich, buttery bread like brioche, and slather the middle with something yummy, like cheese, jam, or Nutella. Then you dip that sandwich into a custard base made with egg, sugar, and whole milk and cook it in hot butter until the bread is crunchy and golden. Finally, you drizzle it with syrup or powdered sugar and cram it into your mouth with a fork or shovel. It's heavenly.

Here's what *I* did.

For stuffed french toast #1, I put American cheese between slices of Wonder bread and stacked the sandwiches high on a baking sheet—as in, literally on top of one another. Recipe complete.

For stuffed french toast #2, I made cream cheese and raspberry jelly sandwiches with that same magical Wonder bread and stacked those high as well.

Then I put the pan in the oven. To *bake*.

There was not an egg or stick of butter in sight. I essentially warmed up weird sandwiches and thought I was Martha Stewart. When I pulled them out, I noticed they looked a little different from my friend's (but maybe that was a good thing because I did it better?), cut them into triangles, and put them on my fancy platters. Lipstick on an overly confident pig.

An hour later (I die thinking back to how gross they must have gotten by then), the staff meeting started. I sat in the back of the room and drew zero attention to myself, not out of embarrassment but because I didn't want my fellow staff members to know that I *wanted them to know* I was responsible for this culinary masterpiece.

I sat at a table, watching my friends and coworkers line up for breakfast, "humbly" waiting for the praise to pour in.

I don't need to tell you that it did *not*.

Breakfast was disgusting. I mean, really and truly disgusting. I could sense not only the disappointment in the room but also the awkward game of social hot potato as people tried to thank the mystery cook for a breakfast they would later need to supplement with granola bars.

Maybe I was dramatic to almost quit my job over this fiasco, but that response mostly checks out. I was humiliated. I had tried to be impressive, to show everyone I could do it all: set a perfect table, make a perfect meal, and receive compliments with perfect humility. Instead, I probably gave somebody food poisoning. *I cared too much about the wrong things.*

In case you're wondering, this is definitely *not* how to think like a Lazy Genius.

TRYING TOO HARD

When you care about something, you try to do it well. When you care about everything, you do *nothing* well, which then compels you to try even harder. Welcome to being tired.

If you're in the second camp, it's likely your efforts to be an optimized human being have fallen embarrassingly short, as have mine. Intellectually, we know we can't do it all, but still we try. Over the last decade of my life, I've done a lot of self-reflection and therapy trying to figure out why being perfect at literally everything felt like the answer.

Everyone's story is different, and mine involves abuse. (Yes, that's abrupt, and now you know I go real deep real fast.) My father and my home life were unpredictable, and as a kid, I learned that my choices had the power to affect my safety. If I stayed quiet, got good grades, and kept my room clean, he wouldn't get mad. While my actions weren't always a direct correlation to his, I lived as if they were. I equated safety with value and love and consequently saw my choices as the only measure of my worth. I thought I needed to be the perfect daughter, student, and friend in order to matter.

I tried so hard to be enough, but my dad didn't stop telling me how to be better. I remember feeling so worthless as a kid, not understanding why he thought I should have blond hair instead of brown, why my straight A's were expected and not celebrated, or why he and my mom were so unhappy. Naturally, I assumed that I was the problem, that I wasn't trying hard enough or being perfect enough to make our home a happy place. The feeling of inadequacy was overwhelming and seeped into my other relationships too.

I was every teacher's favorite student. I did my homework early and without a single mistake. I was the most dependable line leader and class monitor and scored in the ninety-ninth percentile on every standardized test I took. No student is perfect, but I got really close, assuming that was the only way to be loved.

I also tried to be the perfect friend. I didn't rock the boat, I kept my problems to myself, and I was a chameleon in each relationship. No one knew that I was ashamed of having divorced parents, that I desperately wanted to be pretty, or that I was one mistake from falling apart. I assumed letting people see the imperfect, broken parts of me would put the friendship in jeopardy, and that simply wasn't an option.

> That's the irony of perfection: the walls that prevent your vulnerability from being seen also keep you from being known.

That's the irony of perfection: the walls that prevent your vulnerability from being seen also keep you from being known. I was always trying to hide behind perfection because I didn't think my full self was enough. Maybe you feel that way too.

I'm not trying to get into your business, but you likely have shame, fear, or insecurity about something and put forth a lot of effort trying to hide it. We all do because we're all human, and it doesn't have to come from something as dark as childhood abuse. Every story counts, but remember that those stories often come with lies we believe about ourselves. You and I and the pretty stranger at Target all have stories that keep us trying hard at the wrong things, and the harder we try, the stronger the lie.

You're loud and take up too much space.
You're not enough like your sister.
You're too much like your dad.
You're not smart enough, pretty enough, athletic enough.
It's your fault she's gone.

As you get older, those shameful thoughts and feelings don't leave; they just change shape.

You're not a good enough cook.
How dare you not want kids.
You work too much.
You must be doing something wrong if you're still not married.
You're a bad mom for letting your kids watch television.
No one wants to be your friend.

Trying hard to impress others, to hide, or to fight the shame that's annoyingly poking your insides takes up more energy than you can bear. Add laundry and car pools on top of that? I mean, come on.

When trying hard fails you, you seem to be left with one choice: to give up.

NOT TRYING HARD ENOUGH

Shortly after the church breakfast debacle, I threw in the towel. No more being impressive. No more caring. And I went too far. I tricked myself into thinking I had only two options: try too hard or don't try at all. I forgot that trying itself isn't the problem. It's beautiful to try when it comes to things that actually matter, but I definitely embraced the baby-out-with-the-bathwater approach.

Even though one of my greatest joys is loving people by cooking for them, I ordered pizza when friends came over because I thought a homemade meal was trying too hard. Even though a calm and tidy home is good for my hamster wheel of a brain, I left my house in shambles because cleaning up was trying too hard.

> **You don't have to be perfect, and you don't have to give up. You simply get to be *you*.**

I stopped caring and I stopped trying, and somehow I *still* felt tired.

Little did I know you can be just as exhausted from not trying as you can from trying too hard. Managing apathy and survival mode takes as much energy as managing rules and perfection. Still, I leaned into "messy hair, don't care" to hide the fact that I cared deeply. I needed something that stopped the crazy pendulum swing from caring too much about the wrong things to not caring at all.

Thankfully, that's the gift of the Lazy Genius Way. You're allowed to care. You're allowed to know yourself and be yourself—to be real. You don't have to be perfect, and you don't have to give up. You simply get to be *you*.

Stop trying at what doesn't matter, but don't be afraid to try at what does.

Because it *matters*.

THE STRUGGLE ISN'T THE ONLY THING THAT'S REAL

Our culture is obsessed with being real, but we've been using the wrong measuring stick.

As I type these words, my middle son is home with a stomach bug, and he and my daughter are watching television because I'm tired of talking to them. I haven't showered in a couple of days, and I'm in a fight with my husband. If I shared that on Instagram, you might think, *I love her for being so real.*

But what if I shared a day when my kids and I were playing soccer outside, dinner was prepped by four o'clock, and I was wearing makeup? Would I still be real?

Yes, I would, and so would you.

I'm all for letting go of perfection, but we've somehow conflated order with being fake. I do it too. I've seen the cute mom pushing a cart of docile children and full-priced Joanna Gaines items through Target and thought, *Sure, her stomach is flat, her kids are eating cucumbers instead of Goldfish, and she's buying everything I want, but she probably has an eating disorder and credit card debt, so I'm doing okay.**

> **I'm all for letting go of perfection, but we've somehow conflated order with being fake.**

I want to stop judging women who have it together, assuming they have something to hide. I want to stop applauding chaos as the only indicator of vulnerability.

Your struggles and insecurities are not lined up next to mine, pageant-style. We need to stop trying to "out-real" each other. That life is why you and I are tired, and we can let it go.

* If this book had GIF capabilities, Jennifer Lawrence would be rolling her eyes so hard at me right now.

So the next time you find yourself looking for flaws in seemingly perfect people, hoping it'll make you feel better, don't. Telling yourself you're better than someone is just as harmful as telling yourself you're worse. We don't get to measure a person's authenticity based on how real her struggle is. That scale is broken.

Instead, invite people over when your house is dirty *and* when it's clean. Be an amazing mother who sometimes yells at her kids. Enjoy a green smoothie without feeling the need to swear off sweets forever.

You can be real when life is in order *and* when it's falling apart. Life is beautifully both.

BE A GENIUS ABOUT THE THINGS THAT MATTER

I might not know you personally, but I do know this: you care about a meaningful life. We all do. It's part of being human. And in this culture of quick fixes and shortcuts, it's natural to think easy is the goal. But you can't shortcut a meaningful life.

You're not choosing all genius or all lazy; instead, you're a Lazy Genius.

A couple of years ago, I did an episode on *The Lazy Genius Podcast* about baking bread. I received dozens of comments along the lines of "this doesn't sound very lazy." Of course it isn't lazy. Homemade bread *matters* to me. Mixing and kneading the dough by hand, spending an afternoon watching it rise, and engaging in a practice that's been part of humanity for centuries . . . why would I want to shortcut that? But if homemade bread doesn't matter to you, the choice is easy. Shortcut bread and have a nice day.

The Lazy Genius principles will help you learn not only what needs a shortcut but also how to create one. They will teach you how to notice what matters and carve out important space in your day to nurture growth in those areas.

Remember, it's not all lazy or all genius. You get to choose. If you and I engage every priority without a filter of what stays and what needs to move along, eventually we'll be at a crossroads: run ourselves ragged caring about everything or give up and care about nothing.

The Lazy Genius Way offers a different path: be a genius about the things that matter and lazy about the things that don't.

You have permission to let go, wonder, and go slow or to desire, hustle, and power through. Whatever you choose, make sure you're focused on what matters to you, not what matters to Instagram, your mother-in-law, or the voice in your head saying you're not enough.

Every choice matters because each one matters to someone, but hold only the ones that matter to you. As you live as a unique, stunning, powerful individual, embracing what matters and ditching what doesn't, you'll empower the women in your life to do the same.

I'm glad we're in this together.

TO RECAP

- Perfection keeps you safely hidden but also keeps you from being truly known.
- Order isn't always fake, and chaos isn't always vulnerable.
- Be a genius about the things that matter and lazy about the things that don't.
- Use a recipe the first time you make stuffed french toast.

— ONE SMALL STEP —

Smile at the pretty stranger at Target without judging her or yourself. We both know you're going to Target today, so you'll get your shot.

Now let's look at our first principle.

DECIDE ONCE

Lazy Genius Principle #1

I'm not breaking any ground with this statement, but I used to hate Mondays.

Sometimes I would approach them with a lazy "whatever happens, happens" attitude and then cry into my cup of cold coffee as events took place around me.

Other Mondays got a dose of determined genius. I'd spend Sunday night maniacally scribbling in my newest planner, organizing every meal I'd make, glass of water I'd consume, errand I'd run, and hourly Scripture verse I'd recite, only to follow through on basically nothing.

Lazy Mondays didn't work because I didn't know what to do, and genius Mondays didn't work because I gave myself too much to do.*

Then I Lazy Geniused Mondays (and many other challenges) with our first principle: *Decide once.*

---

*Both kinds of Mondays often involved Oreos.

THE EASIEST WAY TO
GIVE YOUR BRAIN A BREAK

The research on it is varied and probably hard to articulate anyway, but we make a lot of decisions. Like, *a lot*. Constant decision-making is one of the reasons you don't have energy for things that matter to you. By discovering a few opportunities to decide once and then never again, you give your brain more room to play.

You might think that making preemptive decisions is robotic, but automation makes you a robot only if you automate everything. Making one-time decisions about what doesn't matter so you have brain space for what does is the Lazy Genius Way, and you'll experience the benefits immediately.

HOW I LAZY GENIUSED MONDAYS
BY DECIDING ONCE

I hated the pressure of Mondays because I felt like every decision reset to zero. Suddenly, nobody in my family knew up from down, breakfast from dinner, or what an appropriate school outfit looked like. Those uncertainties felt fine on a relaxed Saturday but not on a need-to-be-productive Monday.

Since the day itself wasn't going anywhere, I had to change how I approached it, and I started with my outfit. Choosing what to wear uses just a sliver of thinking but a sliver all the same, so I decided once on a Monday uniform and never looked back. Hand to heart, I've been wearing the same outfit every Monday for over three years.*

---

*It's all black and denim. Cold-weather uniform: black jeans and a chambray shirt. Mild-weather uniform: black T-shirt and jeans. Hot-weather uniform: black T-shirt and denim shorts.

I felt the immediate impact of that decision and wanted more. Over time, I kept deciding once—what time I would get up, what I'd do first thing in the morning, what we'd eat for dinner that night. I'll continue to add to the list based on my current stage of life.

Now I adore Mondays because all those fixed decisions give me a beautiful jump start on the day and therefore the week. Instead of being distracted by all the decisions that need making, deciding once consistently gives me time to engage in what matters. I have margin in which to do work I love, read, listen to music, and be patient with my kids as they adjust to a new week of school.

It sounds crazy that a single decision made once can have such an impact, but that's what makes it part of the Lazy Genius Way.

WHERE FIXED DECISIONS ALREADY EXIST

You might not have even realized that you're surrounded by fixed decisions:

- **Fast-food value menus.** The bigwigs decided once what constitutes a meal and put a number in front of it so all you have to do is say "a number two with a Diet Coke."
- **Netflix DVDs in your mailbox.** In the original model, you'd put the movies you wanted to see in a queue, and Netflix would ship you the next DVD so you didn't have to decide what to watch next.
- **Church liturgy.** Responsive readings, communion, and the benediction are fixed decisions that help you

engage in the story of Christ during your Sunday morning worship service.

Deciding once can be done *to* you, but the power comes when you decide once for yourself.

Here's a surprise: every item you own is a fixed decision. When you buy a shirt, a new set of pens, or a gallon of olive oil from Costco, your choice to buy it is also a choice to use, store, and take care of it.

However, when you don't follow through with that choice and leave the shirt in the bag, the pens in a desk drawer you never open, and the gallon of olive oil on the floor of your pantry because it's too big for the shelf, you're adding to the clutter and noise of your life, not the ease and margin that fixed decisions can offer.

> **Every item you own is a fixed decision.**

What's important, then, is to make *good* fixed decisions— ones that will add value to your life instead of taking value from it. Decide once, on purpose, about everything, from the items in your closet to what's on your calendar. A single, intentional decision relieves your brain of effort, freeing you to think about what matters to you instead of living in a cycle of choosing this and that over and over again.

The possibilities are endless, but you don't need endless. Loosen your grip on making thirty-seven decisions by the end of this chapter, thirty-six of which you'll forget by tomorrow. Simply look for one idea that works right now.

Let's run through some life application examples of how to decide once.

DECIDE GIFTS ONCE

Theoretically, you probably love the idea of giving gifts. Oh, to be generous in spirit and in your choice of premium wrapping paper. But realistically, it's a pain. You already struggle to accomplish what's on your regular to-do list, so when gift-giving situations suddenly arise, you feel a twinge of resentment at having to take care of one more thing. Sure, that thought feels icky, but the real truth is that we don't resent giving gifts; we resent not having the margin to be more thoughtful about the process.

You could totally deep-dive all the people in your life and make an exhaustive list of their likes and dislikes, create a spreadsheet of all the potential gift-giving scenarios for the coming year, and do your Christmas shopping in April. If that doesn't make you feel like you live in crazy town, do your thing, girl.

Thankfully, being a Lazy Genius is much simpler. Let's explore some common scenarios.

Gifts for Teachers

If you have kids, they likely have teachers, and you now have many opportunities to be stressed out about getting them gifts. Teacher Appreciation Day, Christmas, and the last day of school are the big three. Multiply that number by how many kids you have, and wow! It's a circus of last-minute Starbucks gift cards and homemade sugar scrubs you don't have time for.

Instead, decide once. Choose now what you'll get every teacher for every occasion. For Christmas, I give a book.* For Teacher Appreciation Day, I give a Target gift card. For the last day of school, I write a heartfelt thank-you note, possibly ac-

---

* *Cozy Minimalist Home,* by Myquillyn Smith, is my current choice.

companied by a drawing or note from my kid. Obviously, you're not restricted to my choices. You can pick your own.

And, hey, I can feel your tension. This sounds like the best idea ever but also like you have no soul if you actually do it. Release that. By intentionally thinking through what would make a great gift ahead of time, you're saving yourself from feeling stressed and resentful and being at the mercy of whatever chevron coffee mug Target has in stock.

Make the decision once and for all.

Birthday Gifts for Your Kids' Friends

The two questions I always ask when we get a birthday party invitation are *Do I have to go too?* and *Do we need to bring a gift?*

The gift question doesn't mean I'm Ebenezer Scrooge. Rather, I'm thinking about all the questions the potential gift raises: Am I contributing clutter to a house that isn't mine? Am I wasting my energy searching for a gift when I'm flying blind on what the kid likes? Am I just going through the motions of a cultural expectation that's rooted in materialism and consumerism? *And where's my cabin in the woods?!*

Every time a random kid needs a birthday present, buy the same one: a puzzle, a book, art supplies, a gift card. My local toy store has a catalog, and I might tuck a gift card inside so the kid can have fun picking out something he wants.

Regardless of what you decide, the point is to decide once. No stressing out when the invitation comes; you already know what to buy.

Gifts for Family Members

You might have an easier time choosing gifts for people you know well, but you still have opportunities to decide once.

The popular "something you want, something you need, something to wear, something to read" is its own form of deciding once when buying gifts for those you love. If limits like that help, use them.

I like to buy my stepdad a book every year because he enjoys reading but doesn't always seek out books on his own, especially when a newspaper is close by. The book changes, but the gift itself is a fixed decision. My little sister is a beauty product whiz, so my new fixed decision is to always get her some kind of skin care product she might not get for herself.*

Wedding and Baby Shower Gifts

The deciding has been done for you; it's called the gift registry. The recipient is showing you exactly what she wants. Some people think buying from a registry is impersonal, but so is running an extra errand . . . which is what returning your gift will be. I feel your offense from here, and I'm not saying you're a trash person because you buy something with a more personal touch.

Balance out your impersonal registry gift with something personal. For a baby shower, get that pack of onesies and include your kids' favorite book from when they were little. For a wedding shower, get the serving bowls the couple picked out and share some handwritten recipes of favorite things to put in those bowls, maybe wrapped up in a pretty tea towel you think they'll like.

DECIDE WHAT YOU WEAR ONCE

I already mentioned my Monday uniform. Getting dressed on a Monday always felt stressful simply because I didn't want to

---

*Sorry, Hannah—spoiler alert.

make an extra decision, which is why my Monday uniform has been such a gift.

In fact, I've been tempted to take it even further after hearing a story about a guy who has a daily uniform. He found his perfect pair of pants and bought three. He found his perfect black T-shirt and bought seven. He wears the same pair of black shoes until they fall apart and then buys another as a replacement. This dude even has multiple pairs of his favorite underwear and socks, all in black.

His outfit possibilities are blissfully limited, and I'm so into it.

Understandably, deciding once to such an extreme feels intense. But it's also beautiful. This guy decided what he likes to wear and wears it every day. The mental energy needed to get dressed each morning is nonexistent. This one decision even spills over into how he does laundry, how and where he stores his clothes, how he packs for a trip, and how he adjusts his clothes based on the weather.

You don't have to wear the same thing every day to see the benefits of how one fixed decision can lead to more.

Take getting dressed for a wedding. What if you chose two dresses to wear, one for warm weather and one for cold? You wouldn't wonder if you'll be comfortable or if you'll have to wear Spanx. You could choose dresses that could be dressed up or down based on the formality of the wedding by tailoring your shoe and jewelry options.

Now, hear me. I'm not saying you should have only two dresses and all black clothes or, God forbid, no superfluous shoes. This is not the point.

The point is you have an opportunity to create fixed decisions in areas of your life that feel stressful. Do you love getting dressed up for a wedding because you usually wear jeans and a T-shirt? By all means, take your time deciding from a million options if it brings you genuine joy.

Decide what to wear once only if it works for you.

IS A CAPSULE WARDROBE WORTH THE HASSLE?

A capsule wardrobe is not for everyone, but here's where the concept is helpful to us all: every item you own is a fixed decision.

When you buy something, you're deciding it's worth choosing over and over again. You're deciding to give it space—in your closet and your mind.

If your closet is full of items that aren't worth choosing, they're taking space away from the items that matter and make you feel like yourself.

Keep in your closet only fixed decisions you're happy making, no matter how many items you have or how well they go together.

DECIDE WHAT YOU EAT ONCE

Mealtime is another opportunity to decide once. Stuffed french toast notwithstanding, I love cooking and being in the kitchen. Feeding people matters to me, but that doesn't mean it's without stress.

Rather than being all lazy with no plan or all genius but a food robot, I'm a Lazy Genius by making the stressful parts easier with a few fixed decisions. I'd love to share some of my ideas.

Use the Same Ingredients

My biggest stressor is seemingly limitless options. I want every ingredient, every new cookbook, and the time to make every new recipe I can get my hands on. Oh, and I want kids who will eat every bite without complaint.

Fat chance.

Instead of being at the mercy of both endless possibilities and my children, who fancy themselves food critics, I decided once that I'd cook only from a fixed list of ingredients. For example, the only fish we eat is salmon. For now, we skip shellfish. On the vegetable front, we eat carrots, potatoes, green beans, corn, and several others, but we currently pass on artichokes, leeks, and squash. Certain foods* on the list often get turned down at the dinner table, but that surprises no one. As my kids broaden their palates and I find more margin in the kitchen and the budget, I'll expand the list.

And remember, I'm not limiting my ingredient list because I hate food. I love it deeply, perhaps more than a human should love a collection of inanimate objects. And because I love it, I want my experience in the kitchen, especially in this Tiny Human Stage, to be as pleasant as possible. Limiting my ingredients does that for me.

Bonus: making my ingredient list a fixed decision has made other decisions easier too. Choosing new recipes is a breeze because I skip any that have ingredients not on my list. Shopping is a breeze because I buy the same things over and over. Putting away groceries is a breeze because I don't have to make room for unfamiliar items.

* By "certain foods," I clearly mean green ones.

Deciding once is a breeze maker. Let's explore other possibilities that make cooking and eating easier.

Make the Same Meal When You Have People Over

Inviting new people over can feel scary, so make it easier by offering the same meal each time. Choose a crowd-pleasing recipe you feel confident making, and always serve it the first time someone comes to your home. Now you can enjoy being hospitable rather than stressing out over what to have or how it's going to turn out. Homemade pizza is my personal go-to. I love making it for new friends because it's fun and everybody likes pizza.*

Create a Meal Matrix

A meal matrix is a way to decide once what you'll eat on certain days of the week. Meatless Monday, Taco Tuesday, and Instant Pot Wednesday are all forms of deciding once.

At my house, we always have Pasta Monday, Pizza Friday, and Leftovers Saturday. My choices within those categories are open, but I've already made a helpful choice.

The nice thing about a meal matrix is that it's completely customizable. You don't need me to tell you what to decide once; you can make your own choices and plug them in where they make sense. You don't have to be overly specific with any day or even have every day filled. Three days are enough for me; fewer or more might work better for you.

Regardless, deciding your meal matrix once creates an easy, actionable meal planning system that's the perfect combination of lazy and genius.

---

* Just be sure everyone eats dairy and gluten. It's sad to serve pizza to someone who can't eat it. Ask me how I know. (Sorry, Lindsay!)

Streamline Grocery Shopping

This suggestion doesn't work for everyone's budget, but if you hate grocery shopping, pick one store you like and skip the others, no matter what the sale flyers say.

We forget that time and sanity are valuable too. Ignoring them for the sake of the lowest price could have bigger consequences than saving a buck on Tater Tots.

Decide once where you shop.

You could also decide once that you'll shop one time each week, that you won't try new brands during this busy season

THE LAZY GENIUS WAY TO DECIDE WHAT'S FOR LUNCH

- *Make a pot of soup on Sunday for a week of lunches.*

- *Make several salads-in-a-jar at once.*

- *Buy lettuce and a favorite cheese to make your sandwiches actually taste good.*

- *Choose a meal that doesn't get traction at dinner because of picky kids, and eat it for lunch instead. Do that meal-prep thing in cute glass containers to make it more fun.*

- *Pick one easy recipe that you'll keep making for lunch until you get tired of it. Then choose another. No need to stress out by reinventing the lunch wheel.*

of life, or that you'll always do curbside pickup and risk a bruised banana or two.

We create unnecessary stress by remaking decisions about how we shop every time we need food, so find a way to decide once and lower the stress.

DECIDE HOW YOU CLEAN ONCE

I loathe cleaning, and regardless of whether you share my hatred, deciding once can help the entire process feel manageable.

Streamline Your Products

When you buy a cleaner that's on sale, a fancy microfiber cloth, or a magic mop you saw on *Shark Tank,* you're making a fixed decision to use that item. If you use it and it adds value to your life, high five. If you don't use it, it becomes clutter.

Stuff is the enemy of clean, and the more stuff you have, the harder it is to clean your house. Ironically, when I'm discontented with my home, I buy things to make it prettier or cleaner, which only makes the problem worse by adding to the noise.*

Try buying cleaning products like they're good fixed decisions. If you buy a kitchen spray, use it. If you buy a fancy mop, use it. If you buy a toilet brush, clean the toilet with it and live your life (no matter how magical, it will not make cleaning the bathroom any better).

Streamline your products by choosing the bare minimum for your most necessary jobs. Don't force yourself to choose among

---

* Raise your hand if you have no fewer than four unopened Method spray bottles crammed in a cabinet somewhere because they were on sale at Target and they're so pretty.

five different cleaners like you're scrolling a Netflix queue of disinfectants. Pick up a bottle and go clean. You don't need to waste time choosing something when you can decide once.

Streamline Your Routine

Vacuum on Thursdays. Clean the mirrors when you dust. Clean the shower before you get out. Clean the toilet before you shower because toilets are gross. Your cleaning routine doesn't have to be elaborate, be based on days of the week, or even be a routine at all. Deciding once simplifies cleaning, period.

Pause and think about the cleaning tasks that sap you dry. What would happen if you made one decision just one time to make the process a little bit easier?

DECIDE TRADITIONS ONCE

Every time I hear someone talk about a tradition, like vacationing in the same place every summer or making Christmas cookies the first weekend of December, I get inspired and also super bummed that I don't do any of those things.

But guess what? Traditions are fixed decisions. Rather than overthinking traditions as family touchstones that will live on in memory for years and years, consider how they're really just fun experiences you decided once.

Decide once to go out for pancakes the night before the first day of school. And if everyone digs it, do it again the next year.

Decide once that you'll spend Christmas Eve looking at Christmas lights in your pajamas, and then pile in the car.

Decide once to do a big puzzle as a family after you've eaten Thanksgiving dinner.

We put so much pressure on traditions because we long

AN ANECDOTE: WHEN TRADITION BLOWS UP IN YOUR FACE

Our family always gets together for dinner when it's someone's birthday, and my mom makes whatever meal that person likes. For as long as I can remember, my little sister, Hannah, got boiled shrimp and cocktail sauce as the cornerstone of her birthday dinner.

It was tradition.

Years later, for some forgotten reason, I was in charge of making her birthday dinner instead of Mom. I said to her, "So, what do you want to eat with your boiled shrimp?"

She paused, took a deep breath, and said, "I actually don't like shrimp."

I'm sorry, what?

Decades' worth of shrimp dinner memories filled my head. For her entire life, my sister engaged in a tradition she didn't even like.

Sure, this could be a lesson about not being afraid to say what you love, but it's more a reminder to not go throwing yourself into fixed decisions dressed as traditions that not everyone is jazzed about. This is your PSA.

PS: Our family now has a verbal cue to start conversations that might make everyone feel a little awkward.

We say, "I have a shrimp situation."

for the connection they provide, but we complicate the path to get there. Make a choice once and try it out.

You may have started a tradition.

• • •

Now it's time to decide something—*just one thing*—once. As you put this principle into practice, you'll be pumped about how much mental energy you have to be a genius about the things that matter and lazy about the things that don't.

TO RECAP

- Limit your decisions by making certain choices once and then never again.
- Deciding once doesn't make you a robot but leaves more time for you to be human.
- You can decide once in any area, including giving gifts, getting dressed, making meals, cleaning the house, and creating traditions.

— ONE SMALL STEP —

Name something that stresses you out, and make one fixed decision to make it easier. One, not thirty-seven.

And that is the perfect segue into our next Lazy Genius principle: start small. You might have already grabbed a pen and started writing down all your fixed decisions, but before you burn a hole in your paper, read the next chapter.

START SMALL

Lazy Genius Principle #2

I'm not exactly what you'd call an athlete. I was always picked last for dodgeball, I was a cheerleader who couldn't do a cartwheel, and I was a benchwarmer for my homeschool volleyball team.*

On paper, that's no big deal. We all have different skills, and mine do not involve speed or hand-eye coordination. Intuitively, I knew my worth was based on more than how skinny or strong I was, but the influence of my aforementioned not-awesome dad, television commercials, and the social constructs of high school and college were stacked against me. Thin, pretty girls got attention. Girls like me didn't.

As I explained earlier, a Lazy Genius is a genius about the things that matter—and for far too long, I spent energy on things that *didn't*: the shape and size of my body.

In high school, I went full-on lazy and hid. I wore baggy overalls and had an atrocious haircut, both with the hope that

---

*Yes, homeschoolers have sports teams. We played against tiny Christian schools and had to wear enormous shorts because bare thighs were scandalous. It was a weird time.

no one would bother to look at me. It worked, because most of my friends, guys and girls alike, nicknamed me Mom.*

When it was time to go to college, I swung the other direction and tried to be a genius about my body. I restricted myself to eight hundred calories a day. Not eighteen hundred. *Eight* hundred. In an attempt to develop muscles, I went to the rec center every day and used the leg machines so improperly that I irrevocably screwed up the cartilage in my knees.† I constantly wondered if what I was wearing made me look pretty or if I was just a girl trying too hard.

Despite the fact that my perception of my body was horribly distorted, neither lazy nor genius did me any favors in my attempts to deal with it. Not caring and caring too much leave you in the same place.

Stuck.

THE PROBLEM WITH GO BIG OR GO HOME

We could be talking about body image, marriage, or closet organization, but our reaction to many problems is to either try harder or give up. Be all in or all out. Go big or go home.

We wait for our life stage to change completely, our kids to grow up, our marriages to improve, our homes to be bigger, our bodies to be smaller. We don't invite anyone over for dinner because our house isn't right yet, we don't know how to cook anything, and we can't figure out how to put flowers in a vase without it looking like a preschooler did it.

---

*I love being a mom now, but when you're sixteen, that's a devastating nickname to get from guys you think are cute. *Devastating*.

†I will never forget being nineteen and hearing the doctor say, "You have the knees of a seventy-year-old woman." I went from Mom to Grandma before the age of twenty. Awesome.

We can't do it all, so we don't do anything.

Stuck.

Or we use arbitrary fresh starts like January 1 to construct an A-to-Z system in our homes, our work, and our bodies, expecting immediate results and going full Hulk when we don't see them. And then we quit and try the next idea.

Also stuck.

We think, *Well, maybe it hasn't worked yet because I haven't found the right system!*

Nope. The right system is irrelevant if you haven't yet named what matters and is especially irrelevant if you dismiss the value of small steps.

Small steps get you unstuck.

WHY SMALL STEPS MATTER

You probably think small steps are a waste of time, and for a while, I was right there with you. I believed small steps don't show big results quickly enough. I saw them as pointless and frustrating and thought, *Shouldn't I be disciplined enough to do more than this one tiny thing?*

One image that helped me view it differently comes from social reformer Jacob Riis: "When nothing seems to help, I go and look at a stonecutter hammering away at his rock, perhaps a hundred times without as much as a crack showing in it. Yet at the hundred and first blow it will split in two, and I know it was not that last blow that did it—but all that had gone before."[1]

Movement, not necessarily a finish line, is the new goal.

We don't give enough credit to all that goes before, but that's precisely why small steps matter: they're doing invisible work, and we can trust that process.

You've probably had someone from an older generation tell you "There's no substitute for hard work" or "If something is worth doing, it's worth doing well." True enough. But we assume, then, if we're not sweating because of it, we're not benefiting from it. That goes for exercise, doing laundry, and combating loneliness. If we're not working excessively hard to make something happen, we might as well give up until we can put forth the effort required.

That might be how a genius approaches goals and growth, but a Lazy Genius starts small.

Small steps are easy.

Easy steps are sustainable.

Sustainable steps keep moving.

Movement, not necessarily a finish line, is the new goal.

MAKE SURE THE END IS WORTH THE MEANS

Even if you're still a fan of the finish line, make sure it's one that actually matters to you. Do any of these scenarios sound familiar?

- You think you should exercise more, but you're doing it to get skinny because you think skinny people have more value.
- You're a working mom, and you bust your butt to make dinner at home every night because you believe that moms who cook are more valuable than moms who don't.
- You're insecure about the fact that you never went to college, so you set ridiculous goals for how many books you'll read because you think it'll make you smarter and therefore more valuable.

I'm not saying you have to give yourself a therapy session every time you make a decision to change some part of your life, but if you keep trying at something that feels like an emotional hamster wheel, maybe it's worth looking at why you're doing it in the first place. If your motivation depends on something that doesn't truly matter to you, you'll wear yourself out trying too hard or simply stall out again.

Take small steps toward something that matters, and stop getting stuck.

SMALL STEPS MATTER EVEN WHEN THE END *IS* WORTH THE MEANS

I'm high-strung and inflexible (both mentally and physically), and yoga is a no-brainer for an aching back and caffeinated-squirrel brain. So for most of my thirties, I went big in making yoga a regular part of my life. My finish line—mindfulness and a body that wasn't always tight and sore—mattered to me. All I had to do was make it happen.

I attempted the whole "I'm going to do yoga for thirty minutes four times a week" thing, but I never once made it all four days. To find my way, I downloaded apps. I bought the mat and the blocks and the eggplant-colored workout top. I had checklists and phone alarms. I even bought a pass for ten hot yoga classes.*

Nothing worked. I could not make four thirty-minute yoga sessions happen weekly no matter how hard I tried, and it was beyond frustrating. I wanted to learn yoga! My reason really mattered! No one was forcing me! Why was this so hard?

---

*If you want to feel like you have no control over your life, start your big fat yoga journey at a hot yoga class, where you sweat like a linebacker for ninety minutes and then can't drive home because your legs feel like they might be broken. It's super fun.

Because it was too *big*.

Even if you're moving toward a goal that does matter, small steps are still your best bet because you'll actually *move*. If instead you put too much pressure on yourself with a big system, you'll spend more time tending to its maintenance than actually gaining momentum.

A life of meaning doesn't happen in one fell swoop but in small, intentional decisions day after day. It's tended to and cared for. Shortcuts don't always work, and big systems are even less effective.

Small steps matter and are easier to keep taking.

WHEN SMALL STEPS FEEL RIDICULOUS

On January 1 last year, I thought about my goals the way every red-blooded American does at the start of a new year, and I knew my approach to yoga had to be different from before. If I wanted to practice yoga on a regular basis, I had to start so small it was embarrassing.

My commitment? One down dog pose a day.

Just one.

If you're unfamiliar with yoga, a down dog is a pose where your hands and feet are both (ideally) placed flat on the ground and your butt is in the air. It's how you'd make the letter A with your body in a game of charades. And with the exception of corpse pose (where you lie on the ground like a dead person), it's about the easiest yoga pose there is.

Every day, I did one down dog. I bent over, put my hands on the ground and my butt in the air, held the pose for a couple of deep breaths, and then stood up again. Done for the day.

Obviously, I felt like a moron going on this laughably low-stakes adventure, but I was determined to stick it out to see if this approach might actually do something. Going big hadn't worked, so maybe going small would.

For a while, the answer—at least from a results perspective—was a resounding no. I didn't automatically become more flexible, and I was not at all what you'd call Zen. Still, my routine was too small to quit, so I didn't.

Huge win.

I did my pose in the morning or before bed if I'd forgotten to do it earlier, and sometimes I'd do both. Occasionally, I'd do an entire sun salutation (a connection of a dozen poses that includes a down dog), which still took no more than fifteen seconds.

After about four months, I had gradually built upon that first small step and was now doing yoga maybe thirty seconds a day.

I repeat: thirty seconds a day.

Sure, if I thought about it from a genius perspective, the whole thing felt foolish. What a joke to think thirty seconds of yoga meant anything. Luckily, I had a Lazy Genius perspective that was much more encouraging. I had developed a *daily habit of yoga,* and despite the fact that it lasted only as long as a beer commercial, I was really proud.

I was moving in the direction of something I'd always wanted.

Small steps were working.

DO SMALL STEPS ACTUALLY COUNT?

Internet foodie Bri McKoy didn't have long afternoons to sit down with a book but still wanted reading to be part of her daily life. Instead of forcing large chunks of time where there weren't any, she started small by reading for ten minutes a day before making dinner. Just ten minutes. Often, that's not long enough to finish one chapter, but she knew it was a small, doable step that would make her a reader. Not *become* a reader . . . *be* one.

You might think if you don't build it big, it doesn't count. I can't say I do yoga every day when I'm doing only one pose, can I? Yes, I can, and you can say it about whatever step you decide to take too.

The smaller the step, the more likely you'll do it. The more you do it, the more you'll *keep doing it,* making it a meaningful part of your daily rhythm, which is what counts.

Yes, I do yoga. Yes, Bri is a reader. Yes, you can claim your goal even if you're doing small steps.

Now, if I walk around the block each day, can I call myself a marathon runner? No, because I've never run a marathon. This is why being a Lazy Genius and naming what matters to you is important.

If you want to call yourself a painter but your mental finish line is owning a studio or making a living from your work, you're naming the wrong goal. You don't have to be a professional; just be a person who paints.

When you start big, you can never get big enough. If you think big is the only measure that counts, you'll keep changing the stakes and moving the finish line.

Be a Lazy Genius and embrace the power of small steps. They matter, they count, and they're the best way to start moving.

WHEN THE ROCK FINALLY BREAKS

Fourteen months into my small daily yoga practice, all I had to show for it was just that—a small daily yoga practice. I felt a tiny bit more flexible and liked the feeling of my back crack-ing when my arms stretched high in the morning, but I couldn't stand on my head or cut you with my calves. I was ordinary and still couldn't get my feet flat on the ground when doing the down dog. My body-charades letter A was always a little bit crooked.

Then one night while I doing my yoga before bed, I started the sun salutation and realized something had changed. All of a sudden, my feet were flat on the ground during the down dog. I could hold low plank (which is basically a pushup be-fore you push up) for a solid five seconds without shaking. I was in the flow you want to be in with yoga. My breath sud-denly matched my movements naturally, without my having to think about it. It was such a fun Saturday night.

I had been diligently taking this incredibly small step for fourteen months. *Fourteen months.* In the past, if I didn't see results in fourteen *days*, I'd usually quit. And the great irony is that I made progress—not only in my commitment to a daily yoga practice but also in the physical practice itself—and it didn't take four hours of weekly yoga to get there. It simply took the same small step day after day.

I'd rather take the same small step every day for fourteen months and experience what matters than go big and stay stuck.

If you want to be a genius about what matters and lazy about what doesn't, you have to embrace small steps.

Small steps are easy.

Small steps are sustainable.

Small steps help you actually move, which is half the bat-tle, considering your other options are to try harder or give up.

The smaller the step, the more likely you'll take it and the more often you'll engage in what matters to you.

As you notice the effects of one choice, you'll start noticing the power of *single choices*. One choice definitely makes a difference in your day, and, as the stonecutter experienced, days filled with singular choices make a difference in your life.

PRACTICAL WAYS TO START SMALL

Want to take vitamins every day? Put the bottle on the counter each morning.

Want to cook dinner every night? Start with Tuesdays.

Want to develop a cleaning routine? Wipe off the kitchen counter each night before bed.

Want to take walks more often? Put your shoes by the door as a reminder.

Want to have a thriving business? Reach out to one potential client a day.

Want to feel like a person? Want to remember the truth of who you are? Spend a minute each day taking deep breaths on your front step.

TO RECAP

- Not caring and caring too much both leave you stuck, but small steps help you get moving.
- The goal is movement rather than a finish line.
- Small steps are easy; easy steps are sustainable; sustainable steps actually go somewhere.
- Small doesn't mean wasteful—all those single choices add up.

— ONE SMALL STEP —

Name an area in your life that matters but often gets the short end of the stick. Choose an embarrassingly small step you can take to move forward in that area, and then do it every day. It's not a waste because you're still moving.

Small steps teach you to embrace the power of single choices, and our next principle is the easiest, most transformative single choice you can make.

ASK THE MAGIC QUESTION

Lazy Genius Principle #3

The hours after school are a beast. (Can I get an amen?) Inevitably, school pickup happens when a younger sibling is napping. After pickup, everyone is hungry and cranky, you have to be a fun cruise director for unwanted homework, the sun is shining (important for energy and vitamin D but not helpful in trying to get subtraction worksheets done), you have to make dinner, and all you want is a nap.

You know it's coming. The frenzy after school shouldn't be a surprise, yet it still catches you off guard.

Some days I leaned lazy and let the madness happen. Chaos reigned supreme, and I found solace in shouting at my children and consuming a stack of Oreos.

Genius days weren't much better. I made plans for everything except flexibility, which is possibly the most prized item in a parent's toolbox, and lost my mind when something didn't happen according to my carefully crafted schedule.

Lazy or genius alone didn't cut it; by the time my husband got home from work, I usually looked like I came out on the wrong end of a zombie invasion.

I *did,* at least, before the Magic Question became a regular part of my life.

The Magic Question, put simply, is this: *What can I do now to make life easier later?*

TEND TO THE NECESSARY BEFORE IT BECOMES URGENT

Not using the Magic Question is like playing Whac-A-Mole.

In Whac-A-Mole, you respond to the urgent. One wrinkly brown face pops into view, and you focus on knocking it back down. But while you deal with that mole, out pops another. Soon, you're randomly pounding the machine and hoping for the best.

You're creeped out by how familiar that sounds, aren't you?

You feel crazy because everything is happening at once: everyone needs you right now, the dryer is buzzing, the car is out of gas, the permission slip is due, and you still haven't decided what's for dinner.

The Magic Question is more like playing dominoes. And by that I mean setting them up in a row to be knocked over one by one.* Think of the Magic Question as the first domino in line. Ask yourself, *What can I do now to make life easier later?* And follow through on that one thing. Rather than responding to the next urgent issue that pops up, you make one simple choice, which leads to another, and the decisions you face begin to fall into a more predictable order.

Remember, Lazy Geniuses start small.

You don't need to tackle a dozen tasks to prepare for later; begin with one.

---

*I've been told there's an actual game with points, but I live with elementary school boys. We just have dominoes to knock them over.

You might think more is better, but you'd be wrong. When you throw more at the problem, you're trying to eliminate the urgent altogether, which is comically impossible. Instead, your goal is to stay one step ahead so you're not putting out fires as part of your daily rhythm. We've all gotten burned plenty of times and will again, but you can be better prepared by asking that one magical question: What can I do now to make life easier later?

Once you start asking, you'll never want to stop. Let's look at some ways you can change your life with this one simple question.

MAGIC QUESTION CASE STUDY #1: AFTER SCHOOL

What can I do now to make the after-school schedule easier later?

My favorite answer is a snack platter. Before I leave to get my boys from elementary school, I pull out a big ol' plate and pile it high with whatever food I can find. Crackers, carrot sticks, pepperoni slices, grapes, a big chocolate chip cookie broken into chunks . . . whatever I have. I set the plate on the kitchen table, and it's like a beacon of light when we get home.

The singular choice of a snack platter starts a happy domino effect for the entire afternoon. Instead of exercising their debate skills on why ice cream sandwiches should be considered a fruit, my kids have a platter of different foods they can choose to eat or not eat without argument. They're more eager to put away their backpacks and wash their hands because they don't want last pick of the chocolate chip cookie chunks. We connect over clementines and cheese cubes, which helps them settle into the comfort of home after a dizzying day at school.

The transition to homework is easier, too, since we're already at the table and their blood sugar has leveled out. I might even Magic Question dinner a little while they're all occupied filling water cups and divvying up pepperoni.

Do I make a snack platter every day? Nope. But the days I do are easier. That doesn't mean the days I don't are always hard, but it's rare that a snack platter day results in Hulk Mom showing up. That's the thing with the Magic Question: it doesn't guarantee a particular outcome, but, man, it comes awfully close.

MAGIC QUESTION CASE STUDY #2: DINNER

What can I do now to make dinner easier later?

This version of the Magic Question is extra sparkly simply because we eat every single day and can see the payoff more clearly. Dominoes fall so smoothly in the kitchen.

The first time I filled a pot with water for spaghetti four hours before dinner, I remember thinking I was a little crazy. How much help would that actually be? My toddler can fill a pot with water! Then five o'clock hit, and that same toddler became a parasite and would not let go of me. I remember tearing up because I was so glad to turn a knob on the stove rather than try to haul a full pot with one hand while holding a diva two-year-old in my other arm.

Then I watched the next domino fall.

Since the pot of water was already waiting for me on the stove, I wasn't as stressed out by the kid clinging to my body, whom I had to carry to the pantry to get tomatoes. While I was there, I noticed the package of spaghetti and figured it would make later easier if I went ahead and pulled that out too, all with a pigtailed head resting on my shockingly relaxed shoulder.

It may seem small, but one tiny choice can make a massive difference. Mine started with a pot of water.

Let's look at more answers to this particular Magic Question.

Decide What's for Dinner

A huge way to make dinner easier later is to actually know what you're having before dinnertime hits. Decide what's for dinner in advance so you can get what you need at the store. Make a grocery list and tape it to your back door so you'll remember to go to the store in the first place. The answer to the dinner Magic Question doesn't have to be a cooking task; it can simply be a decision.

Prep a Recipe

Let's say you're having chili for dinner. Anticipate what you can do now by thinking through the steps of the recipe. You can put the cans of beans and tomatoes on the counter. (Yes, I put beans in my chili. Don't look at me like that.) You can tear open the spice packet or mix up some chili powder and cumin yourself. You can dice the onion and garlic, put the dutch oven on the stove or plug in the Instant Pot, and pull bowls out of the cabinet so little kids can more easily set the table. Even one of those actions will limit the bandwidth needed during the busy dinner hour.

If you have the margin to do all of them? Stop it. Angels will sing.

Do Common Tasks

If your family eats rice with a lot of meals, go ahead and make a pot. It'll likely get eaten. And if it won't get eaten soon, freeze it. Wash vegetables, pull out your cutting board, or season the chicken you bought on sale. No matter what meal you're having, those tasks will make dinner easier later.

Make a Shopping List

Are you always forgetting to buy certain things when you go to the store? Make dinner easier later by creating a list so you always have what you need.

Make the list-making easier later by putting a whiteboard on your fridge and writing down "soy sauce" the first time you think of it. Then, when you leave for the store, don't worry about copying the list to a piece of paper; take a photo with your phone and head out. You made a shopping list, and dinner is now easier.

I could fill this entire book with answers to the dinner Magic Question, but I'll spare you my culinary geekery. Just know that the world is your oyster. (Or your chicken, if you don't like oysters.)

MAGIC QUESTION CASE STUDY #3: LAUNDRY

What can I do now to make laundry easier later?

Oh, laundry. It's trying to kill us one pile at a time, but the Magic Question can help.

You can buy divided laundry baskets so sorting is done in real time. You can teach your kids how to pull their pants off from the ankles rather than stripping down as if they're in a hazing ritual so you don't find yourself in a whirlwind of inside-out pant legs and *Minecraft* underwear.

A *Lazy Genius Collective* blog reader once shared that she uses a mesh garment bag for her kids' socks. The bag hangs next to the laundry basket, the kids put all their dirty socks there, and the socks get washed and dried in the bag, making sock pairing so much easier later.

Even choosing the day of the week you'll wash a load of clothes can help. If a decision reduces stress later, make it happen, even if it's as simple as "I'll do some laundry on Wednesday."

MAGIC QUESTION CASE STUDY #4: COMING HOME FROM VACATION

What can I do now to make coming home from vacation easier later?

As much as we love traveling, it's always nice to come home—unless the house was left in shambles from the packing frenzy. Here are some ways to make your return a little more joyful.

Tidy Up Before You Leave

If a tidy house calms you, make coming home easier by tidying up before you leave. Restrict the kids to the yard, send them for a doughnut breakfast with a spouse or a responsible, licensed sibling, or buckle them in the minivan and take a couple of minutes to reset before you head out. Whatever it takes to get them out of the house, do it, and quickly tidy up so it's peaceful when you come home.

Have a Dinner Plan Before You Get Home

Groceries are scarce after a vacation, so make coming home easier by knowing what's for dinner. Have a meal in the freezer, reserve twenty bucks from the vacation budget to get pizza, or think of something easy as you're driving home.

You could have a meal-kit service delivered or schedule a grocery pickup for when you return. If figuring out dinner after vacation stresses you out, sic the Magic Question on it.

Unpack Right Away

Coming home from vacation is stressful because it feels like you're unpacking from vacation for as long as you were gone. Instead, make coming home easier later by unpacking everything immediately. It will likely take less time than you think and will make your house feel at peace.

One bonus way to make unpacking easier later is to gather all your dirty laundry in one place while you're on vacation. Have a pillowcase or reserved suitcase for everyone's dirty clothes, and when you get home, there'll be no need to sort through a mountain of luggage to get every last sock to wash.

HOW TO USE THE MAGIC QUESTION TO LAZY GENIUS ANYTHING

Hopefully you're seeing the pattern here. If you initially had no concept of how to make life easier later because it seemed too broad an idea and your morning coffee had already worn off, no worries. Simply sub different words relevant to the situation in front of you. You can't be too specific.

> The Magic Question will become a favorite tool in your Lazy Genius Swiss Army knife because it's as effective as it is simple.

You can, however, make it too complicated. The Magic

Question is so life changing that you'll be tempted to use it for everything, but sadly, that puts you back in tired genius robot territory. Try to keep things simple.

For example, I love my morning coffee ritual, but grinding the beans is loud and might wake my kids before I'm ready to say words to them. What can I do now to make my morning coffee easier (and quieter) later? I can grind the beans at night.* I even put water in the kettle, a nice thing for slower mornings when I'm still half asleep.

For a while, though, I pulled out everything I needed for my coffee: the mug, a spoon, the jar of sugar—everything except the heavy cream, which doesn't like being out all night. Maybe it's not a huge deal to fully prep my morning coffee before I go to bed, but it was unnecessary. Getting a spoon in the morning isn't hard, especially when it's on the way to getting the cream. In fact, I unintentionally removed the joy of piddling around with my coffee routine in the dark morning for no other reason than it made me more prepared.

Don't do something unless it's legitimately helpful. Use what works, ignore what doesn't, and don't complicate it.

The Magic Question will become a favorite tool in your Lazy Genius Swiss Army knife because it's as effective as it is simple. One question with one answer shouldn't have such an enormous payoff, but it does. Dominoes fall, and you won't be able to get enough of it.

---

* My coffee snob—I mean *aficionado*—brother-in-law will be so sad that I'm not grinding them right before I brew. At least I'm not drinking Folgers, Luke. Cut me some slack.

MAGIC QUESTIONS

- What can I do now to make vacuuming the floor easier later? *Have a sixty-second family floor pickup and pull the vacuum out of the closet.*

- What can I do now to make writing my blog post easier later? *Collect ideas in a voice memo and put the computer on the kitchen counter for when I'm ready to write.*

- What can I do now to make grocery shopping easier later? *Put my reusable bags by the door and stick a pen on my shopping list so I can cross things out as I buy them.*

- What can I do now to make getting dinner from the freezer easier later? *Label the meals so I'm not stuck playing "What's in This Bag?"*

- What can I do now to make getting the kids to bed easier later? *Locate all beloved stuffed animals before we start brushing teeth so I'm not on a frantic hunt after story time.*

- What can I do now to make paying bills easier later? *Have a basket specifically for time-sensitive mail, and set an alarm on my phone to remind me to go through it every two weeks.*

- What can I do now to make lunch easier later? *Use a drawer in the fridge for sandwich makings so I'm not always digging around for lettuce and cheese.*

- What can I do now to make choosing a recipe easier later? *Flip through a new cookbook and mark with washi tape the recipes I'm most excited to try. When it's time to choose, stick to what's already marked.*

- What can I do now to make a road trip easier later? *Download an app like Along the Way so I can easily find places to eat, use the restroom, and entertain cranky children.*

- What can I do now to make getting everybody out the door for school easier later? *Make lunches the night before.*

- What can I do now to make a kid's birthday party easier later? *Make and freeze cookie dough balls now so all I have to do is bake them the day of the party.*

- What can I do now to make hosting my first Thanksgiving easier later? *Remember that my value is not in how my turkey compares to my mother-in-law's.*

- What can I do now to make shopping at Aldi easier later? *Keep a quarter in that little cubby next to my steering wheel and always put it back after locking up my shopping cart.*

- What can I do now to make taking the kids to the dentist easier later? *Save my Starbucks points for a Grande Starbucks Doubleshot with one pump of Classic Syrup and heavy cream instead of milk. Thank the good Lord Starbucks has a drive-through.*

TO RECAP

- Ask, *What can I do now to make life easier later?*
- Tend to what's necessary before it becomes urgent.
- Get specific with the Magic Question, and Lazy Genius literally anything.

— ONE SMALL STEP —

What's up next in your day? Ask yourself the Magic Question and see what happens.

It's tempting to make *everything* easier, isn't it? While the Magic Question is powerful, it can't fix everything. Next up, let's talk about how to live like a Lazy Genius, even when your season of life is hard.

LIVE IN THE SEASON

Lazy Genius Principle #4

I had my second baby two weeks after my first kid turned two, and I remember nary a thing from those days.* I was stupidly tired and lived in a haze of dirty laundry and food baked in casserole pans, and I'm confident I always smelled like spit-up. Everything from that time blurs together as one big memory of exhaustion.

I didn't like that season of my life and was pumped it would someday be over. In fact, I remember somberly vowing, as if I were a knight in King Arthur's court, that I would never have another baby and therefore never enter that season again. I love that babies exist and will hold yours with great delight, but as far as kid stages go, Baby Stage isn't my favorite. Toddler Stage is an unfortunate second in that race, and they're right next to each other!

I was done. No more babies.

Which is why I had quite the mental breakdown when, four years later, I stood in the dirty bathroom of a kickboxing gym, peed on a stick, and after ten terrifying seconds saw the digi-

---

*Sorry, sweet Ben. The middle child narrative continues.

tal readout that said PREGNANT in the biggest, boldest, most capital letters I'd ever seen.* I sat on a bench in that unfortunate bathroom, paralyzed from the shock.

I was just about to put my youngest in kindergarten. I was on the verge of getting large chunks of time *every day* when I could be completely alone. I had plans with a capital *P,* and a surprise pregnancy definitely didn't fit them. I thought my season of tiny babies was over. When I found out it wasn't, I was honestly devastated.†

THE GUILT OF WANTING SOMETHING DIFFERENT

Living in your season is complicated because we all hold our seasons differently. You have a different personality and different longings than your friends at church, your coworkers, or the women you see on the internet have, so when you're vulnerable about how difficult you find your current season, you open the door for others to feel offended or dismissed in theirs.

The guilt I felt over being sad about my pregnancy was crippling. How dare I grieve a loss that would be a gain to so many other people? How could I in good conscience share my sadness over being pregnant with friends and family who desperately wanted a baby of their own or who had miscarried or lost a kid to cancer or any number of horrible things?

---

*Yes, *I know* a kickboxing gym is a weird place to take a pregnancy test. If I'd known it would be positive, I obviously would've chosen differently.

†Annie, I love you to pieces, and our family needed you. You don't know how to read yet, but if you ever read *this,* we're obsessed with you. Maybe one day you'll find yourself pregnant with a baby and not sure how you feel about it. Don't feel guilty about that, even for a second. Love and confusion can exist in the same place, my girl. You're going to be okay.

It's enough to keep you privately resentful of your season.

This is why thinking like a Lazy Genius is so important. You can desire things that someone else doesn't. You can struggle with something that gives someone else joy. You can care about what matters to you even if it doesn't matter to someone else, and we can all lovingly and compassionately exist together in that tension.

If you move through a hard season of life without naming what matters and what doesn't, you'll be crushed under the weight of other perspectives and expectations of what your season *should* be. For example, working is such a privilege, and lots of other parents would love time away from their kids. But staying at home is also such a privilege, and lots of other parents would love time at home with their kids.

> You can desire things that someone else doesn't. You can struggle with something that gives someone else joy. You can care about what matters to you even if it doesn't matter to someone else, and we can all lovingly and compassionately exist together in that tension.

The difficulty of a season grows stronger and more oppressive if you don't name what matters. Otherwise, you're at the mercy of others' expectations and will either cram your season into another season's box or disengage altogether. You'll try hard or give up.

THE ALL OR NOTHING OF WANTING SOMETHING DIFFERENT

If you're in a challenging season of life, you probably want out.

You may be tired of waiting for whatever sits on the other

side of the longing and feel exhausted by the guilt of longing for something else. Maybe your challenge is a job you hate, kids that make you tired, or no money in the bank. Maybe you're waiting for a spouse, waiting for a divorce, or waiting for an adoption to finally go through.

Frustration with your present circumstances is real and okay, but if you habitually look behind and beyond where you are, discontentment will be an eager companion whispering in your ear: *It will always be this way.*

There's no way out.

How on earth can you do this for another day?

The lazy response is to disengage, to leave the present to its own devices. You avoid the grief, ignore the life lessons, and just put your head down. No one looks at a difficult season and decides, *I want to be miserable until this is over,* but by disengaging, you're still choosing it. The tension between resignation and hope feels like too much to bear, so you simply shut down.

The genius response is to force one season to look like another. You don't like change or letting go, so you grip tightly to the way things were and demand that your current season match it, or else. Maybe you're the well-meaning pregnant woman declaring that you're not going to let a baby change your relationship with your husband. *We're still us,* you silently vow. This is true, but you're now *us* with a baby. And a baby brings big changes.

What do you do with that? How can you deal with the tension of a hard season, of long stretches when you wish life were different, of changes you weren't anticipating?

Thankfully you don't have to disengage or resist.

There's another way: the Lazy Genius Way of living in your season.

IT WON'T ALWAYS BE THIS WAY, BUT IT IS THIS WAY NOW

Living in your season doesn't mean you gloss over where you are and pretend everything is fine and "God has a plan" and "he doesn't give you what you can't handle" and all the other greeting card comments that can feel hollow.

Living in your season doesn't mean trying to change everything to make your current circumstances look the way you wish they did.

Living in your season means letting your frustrations breathe but not be in charge.

I often get questions from blog readers and podcast listeners who want help with a particular situation, and it's almost always rooted in their current season. For example, a mom of two kids on two different travel baseball teams asked me for tips on eating dinner around the table as a family even though they often don't get home from games until after eight.

My answer? This isn't a season for dinner around the table. Accept the frustration of harried dinners, grieve the loss of being at the table together, and don't try to force your new season into a beloved old one.

> **Living in your season means letting your frustrations breathe but not be in charge.**

Another reader was totally overwhelmed with being a mom of tiny babies. She had a two-year-old and a two-month-old and couldn't figure out why she didn't have any motivation to make dinner or stay on top of the laundry or carry on an adult conversation with her husband at the end of the day. She wrote, "I don't know what happened, and I don't know how to fix it." What happened was a new season of life, and there's no fixing it because she didn't do anything wrong.

Neither have you. It won't always be this way, but since it is now, you can learn to live in your season and let it teach you something.

DO THE NEXT RIGHT THING

As you live in your season, embrace being honest about how you feel *and* be willing to learn from what you find. Pay attention to what's in front of you and stop trying to see every possible step ahead.

Emily P. Freeman says to do the next right thing in love,* and I'm telling you, there's not a more powerful mantra for living in your season.

Don't get swept up in what was or what could be. Start small with what's right in front of you.

Do the next right thing. Think the next true thought. Wash one load of clothes and don't resent the other six. Wipe off a single kitchen counter. Open a window. Call a friend (and promptly tell her no one is dead when she picks up because that's what we all think when a friend calls us these days).

Start small.

Sure, your difficult season of life won't always be this way, but when it *is* this way, pause. Instead of forcing yourself into a more palatable set of emotions or ignoring your longings, be aware and gracious. See your season as an invitation to be human, to name what matters, and to strengthen who you already are.

---

*She wrote an entire book about this subject, *The Next Right Thing*, and it's the kind, wise big sister to *The Lazy Genius Way*.

You don't have to be afraid of stress or sadness. You don't have to panic when things fall out of order. You don't have to run away from a season of life that seems to require more than you have to give. Staying engaged with the sadness but not letting it dictate your decisions is a practice in being a genius about what matters.

Living in your season reminds you that beginnings, endings, and middles all deserve your attention and kindness and that you don't need to rush through them.

Just do the next right thing.

Like our national treasure Mister Rogers once said, "Often when you think you're at the end of something, you're at the beginning of something else."

Maybe your something else is growing stronger in who you already are, one season at a time.

LEARN FROM NATURE'S SEASONS

I'm writing these words in the middle of March, and spring is loud and proud. Last night, a friend and I had a conversation about suddenly feeling something in the air. We both practice regular rhythms of cleaning and minimizing, yet we still have the same desire to open all the windows, get out the Pine-Sol, and go to town. Spring is here.

Like seasons of life, nature's seasons usher in feelings we don't choose but still have to experience. I could do without both summer and the stressful season of having a newborn, but I still have to live them.

If being present in your season of life feels like catching the wind, engage in the adjacent practice of learning from *nature's* seasons. Experience the rhythms of weather, plants, and holidays. Soon you'll see how embracing the rhythms of nature gives you the vocabulary to embrace your season of life, regardless of which one you're in.

Spring

In spring, new beginnings and new life abound. The days grow longer, the sun feels brighter, and you start noticing things you somehow missed in the winter months, like that layer of dust on your television stand.

Your clothes naturally transition from cold to cool weather, which makes you appreciate what you have (all the love for layers) and purge what you no longer need, usually anything bought in the juniors' section at T.J. Maxx.

Flowers bloom in the yard, and you clear off a previously cluttered surface to make room for a vase of daisies. Birds flutter around your window frames looking for a solid nesting spot, and you find yourself looking outside more often, enjoying the simplicity of leaf and sky and chickadee.

Spring naturally encourages new life, in trees and birds' nests, in your closet and your mind. Lean into the hope of spring and see what it has to teach you.

Summer

Summer is my least favorite season. I'll go ahead and put my flag in the sand on that one. Shaving, sunburn, mosquitos . . . *make it stop.*

But summer has good in it too—most notably, a reminder to play and take your time. Even if you have a nine-to-five job and no longer get summers off, there's still a spirit of play in the air. You relearn what it's like to spend an entire day in the water or at the park. Meals happen according to rumbly stomachs and not so much what the clock says. You visit new places and meander as much as tiny toddler legs will allow.

Somehow the inclination to let people into your home comes more easily. You invite friends over for burgers and beer after work. You eat Popsicles every day and remember how delicious lemonade is. The smell of sunscreen catapults you back to being a kid at the beach, and you try not to yell as you slather it on your impossibly wiggly children.

Summer reminds us how much we love routine *and* that we can survive without it. Lean into the ease of summer and see what it has to teach you.

Fall

Fall brings beloved bouquets of sharpened pencils and the restoration of routine, and the holidays wave from around the corner. Fall gets the most love by the masses because of scarves and boots and pumpkin-spice lattes.

While I love the shift in weather and outfits as much as the next person, fall has a secret underbelly of stress. Everything starts shouting for your attention, and suddenly you're neck deep in the urgent once again. You go from the slow pace of summer to the scheduling gauntlet of fall, and it's easy to quickly feel like you're drowning.

Yet all seasons have something to teach us if we pay attention, and fall is the perfect time to decide what matters in your schedule and on your to-do list. You can't possibly do everything everyone else is doing, so choose on purpose. Use the natural rhythm of the season to give you permission to let go of what's bogging you down so you can put your energy into being a genius about what really matters.*

* Fall is also a great time to eat food out of bowls and learn to make bread. Not a rule, just a seasonal suggestion, if you're into that kind of thing.

Lean into the frenzy of fall and see what it has to teach you.

Winter

Winter has two sides.

There's Before Christmas Winter that's jolly and sparkly, full of presents and promise. Hanging out with friends, baking cookies, watching *The Muppet Christmas Carol* for the seventh time. . . . Sure, it's busy but worth it for the fun.

Then there's After Christmas Winter. The sparkle is replaced by boredom brought on by the confining cold, Christmas gifts that have already been rejected, and guilt over New Year's resolutions lying dusty and unmet.

You can embrace and learn from both. Exciting holidays remind you of the sacredness of family and tradition, the magic of celebrations, and the perfection of Christmas music. The long stretch on the other side has the calm you need after all that celebration. You can accept the quiet and darkness as a gift to slow down, turn in early, enjoy slippers and robes and mugs warm and full. You can enjoy what winter offers and feel an even greater appreciation for spring when she gets her turn again.

Lean into these contrasts of winter and see what they have to teach you.

SEASONS ARE BIGGER THAN YOU ARE

When you're longing for a season of life to make sense or wishing it would be on its merry way, nature kindly offers reminders and rhythms, not answers and rigid plans. Winter, spring, summer, and fall help you remember not only where you are but also that where you are is not all there is.

So often, I try to create a system to get through a challenging season of life, and the natural world responds, *Dude, I've
been cycling through life and death for a while now. I understand change, so let's be here together.*

The sun rises.

The snow falls.

The baby starts kindergarten.

The parent passes away.

The job transfer happens sooner than you expected.

The kid who once thought you were everything doesn't talk
to you much anymore.

The husband who chose you changes his mind.

I'm not trying to bring you down, but life is hard. You're
wounded and tired and have stories no one knows, just like I
do and just like the pretty stranger at Target does.

You also might have the tendency to see your circumstances
as the be-all and end-all and forget that so much is happening
within and around you, whether you notice it or not. The more
you focus on what your season doesn't have, the more you'll
despair, compare, resent, and feel generally bummed out. You
also miss out on the good that's right in front of you.

Instead, be where you are.

Do the next right thing.

Live in the season you're in

with open hands so you can re-

ceive what it has to offer.

> **Being a Lazy Genius doesn't
> mean loving every season; it
> means welcoming each one
> kindly and letting it
> teach you something.**

I'm not saying it's easy;
that's a flat-out lie. But seasons
are bigger than you are. They come and go, and they always
invite you to become more of who you already are.

Being a Lazy Genius doesn't mean loving every season; it

means welcoming each one kindly and letting it teach you something.

YOUR SEASONAL PERSPECTIVE

If the mom of the kids on the traveling baseball teams sees this crazy season of life as a loss, as something that doesn't fit into the way things "should be," she'll be grumpy and resentful and wish her kids played chess instead. But if she acknowledges the grief she feels because of the season *and* receives what it might teach her, she'll experience a shift in perspective.

> **Pursuing the ideal forces you to either try harder because your season isn't enough or give up because it will never be enough. Instead, live in your season and be content where you are.**

It's not a season for dinner at home around the table, but it *is* a season for picnics in the back of the SUV between games, for family breakfasts, and for new rhythms of catching up during the ride to school. The situation isn't ideal, but ideal isn't the goal.

Pursuing the ideal forces you to either try harder because your season isn't enough or give up because it will never be enough. Instead, live in your season and be content where you are. Whether you're in the throes of caring for a new baby, waiting for a new job, being at the mercy of your very talented daughter's gymnastics schedule, or simply waiting for the lady in front of you to find exact change, *be content where you are*. Lean into what's happening around you, and don't assume how you live now is how you'll live forever.

Seasons change, and so do you.

TO RECAP

- You can care about what matters to you without feeling guilty.
- Do the next right thing.
- Nature's seasons and your particular season of life all have something to teach you, if you'll live in your season and be content where you are.

— ONE SMALL STEP —

Look out the window. Look at the ground. Look at the sky. Notice what the season wants to teach you in this exact moment. I know that's super annoying advice, but what's more annoying is that it actually helps.

As you learn to live in your season, one of the most helpful tools in your Lazy Genius Swiss Army knife is routine. When your calendar is busy and your inner life feels windswept, it's nice to have the anchor of daily routines to remind you of what matters. In the next chapter, I'll help you create them.

BUILD THE RIGHT ROUTINES

Lazy Genius Principle #5

Fourth grade was a bonkers year for me.

Big change #1: my parents got divorced. My mom had tried to make it work with my dad for my entire childhood, but he often left us for months, sometimes even years, at a time. When I was in fourth grade, he officially quit the family after being gone for two years.

Big change #2: my mom got engaged to a friend she'd met the year before. He's been my stepdad for twenty-eight years now, and he's great. But at the time, I saw him as the guy who was going to try to be my new dad.

Big change #3: I left my school. I had been attending a little Christian school up until this point, the last couple of years on scholarship. It ran out at the end of third grade, so my mom decided to homeschool me, partly because we couldn't afford the tuition, but mostly so she could stay connected with me during the transition gauntlet.

Everyone deals with craziness in different ways, and in case I haven't yet made this clear, my favorite method is to keep things in order. I think that the more I can control, the safer I'll be.

At first, I was grumpy about being homeschooled, but because my mom knew what I needed to get through this transition, she let me be in control. I helped choose my textbooks, I made lists of my assignments and checked them off as I went through each day, and I chose when to have a lunch break. I loved every single bit of it.

The routine of sitting in the same place at the same time every day, working through the same notebooks, and watching the same video while eating the same lunch* was like medicine. The dependability of those days reminded me that I was okay.

That's the gift of a routine: it offers a soft place to land.

THE REAL PURPOSE OF A ROUTINE

Maybe you crave routine to keep some sense of control, and that's okay. Feeling out of control isn't fun, and it's normal to want a safe distance from that emotion.

However, there comes a point when grasping for control makes you feel tired instead of safe. You try to be a genius about routine, making it (and yourself) rigid and robotic. If you don't follow through on your carefully crafted routine, it seems like everything will fall to pieces. Here you are again, trying hard.

> There comes a point when grasping for control makes you feel tired instead of safe.

I'm guessing by this point you already know the lazy way to approach routine: just give up. Routine is for fake people who

---

*The video was an episode of *Kids Incorporated* we recorded onto VHS during a free Disney Channel cable preview, and the lunch was a banana and mayonnaise sandwich, baby carrots, and a chocolate fudge Pop-Tart. Lunch break of kings, my friend.

aren't okay being a mess, so you're going to go with the flow. Besides, you like sleep too much to get up at five for a morning routine, so basically all routine is off the table.

Once again, the Lazy Genius Way is neither of these extremes, thank goodness. Remember that being a Lazy Genius means you're allowed to care about what matters to you, and simple routines can help you do exactly that.

Maybe calm mornings matter, but right now you feel like a shark fighting through a feeding frenzy just to drink your coffee warm. Maybe being in the zone at work matters, but you can't seem to focus on anything but Jimmy Fallon videos. Maybe peaceful evenings with your people matter, but you fall asleep on the couch in the middle of a *Parks and Rec* rerun. Jimmy Fallon and couch naps are lovely things, but if you want to spend your work hours and evenings differently, routines can help.

You might think a routine is nothing more than doing the same things in the same order every day, but that's not the whole story. Routines are meant to lead you into something else.

ROUTINE AS AN ON-RAMP

A morning routine *leads* you into your day. An after-school routine *leads* you and your kids into the onslaught of homework, dinner, and the broken record of children saying, "When can I have screen time?" An evening routine *leads* you into resetting your house or yourself for another day. A work routine *leads* you into a rhythm of activating a different part of your brain and getting stuff done.

> Routines are on-ramps to somewhere else, not destinations themselves.

Routines are on-ramps to somewhere else, not destinations themselves.

If I see my kids' bedtime routine as the destination, I serve the routine instead of the routine serving me. When the routine is in charge, my kids never get to stay up late for holiday fireworks or stick around for the entire family Christmas party.

But what if the routine is simply an on-ramp to a specific purpose? My kids' bedtime routine helps them ease into sleep and feel safe and loved. Those are the destinations that matter.

Though a routine regularly helps us walk the path of what matters, it's not the only road to get there. My kids can ease into sleep wearing pajamas on the drive home. They can feel safe

PEP-TALK HUDDLE

We get weird around the idea of routine, of intentional choices. Someone else's morning routine of getting up at five to read the Bible and exercise and do all the things you think you should *be doing leads to heavy eye rolls on the outside and shame on the inside.*

Regularly embracing a life-giving morning routine doesn't make you better or worse than somebody who hits the snooze button five times or ignores routines altogether. You're allowed to care about what matters to you, and so is everyone else.

Please don't judge others or yourself. Instead, high-five others for living their truth, regardless of how similar to or different from yours it is.

> **Ironically, when you let routine be in charge, you ultimately miss out on what matters anyway.**

and loved by being with their people and having cool experiences outside the norm.

Ironically, when you let routine be in charge, you ultimately miss out on what matters anyway.

If you want to build the right routines, you first need to name where you're going and why that destination actually matters.

WHAT CHRIS HEMSWORTH CAN TEACH YOU ABOUT ROUTINE

Not having a routine is like skydiving, and having one is like surfing.*

With skydiving, there's *in the plane* and *out of the plane.* Sure, there's emotional buildup as you wait for your turn to jump, but there's nothing gradual about the process. In or out. Waiting or screaming your brains out. In real-life terms, that translates to being woken up by a four-year-old jumping on your face.

By contrast, routines are more like surfing.

Chris Hemsworth (you're welcome) is out there in the surf in his wet suit, straddling his board, breathing deeply, and patiently waiting for the next wave. As he sees one forming, he goes through the same motions: paddling on his stomach at first to get in rhythm with the wave and then jumping to his feet once he's caught it.

---

* I've never done either because I'm terrified of both heights and water, but we'll pretend I know what I'm talking about, even though my understanding of both comes from television and Google.

Sometimes the wave is dinky and he falls. Sometimes the wave is enormous and he rides it a long way. Sometimes he loses focus and gets pushed under. No matter the result, the initial process is repeatable and meant to *lead him into something else.*

A routine is a repeatable act of preparation, not the destination.

Ask yourself, *What would I like to be more consistently prepared for? What time of day or specific activity leaves me feeling like I've been pushed out of a plane?*

That's where you build a routine.

HOW TO BUILD A ROUTINE

Now that you know an area where you need a routine and understand its proper context, it's time to build one. Let's go through the steps.

1. Start Small

If you want to be a Lazy Genius about your routine, start with one small enough that you'll actually do it. If you build it big, you won't follow through. Remember how my big yoga plans didn't work but my one measly down dog did? Start small.

When you learn to surf, you don't even start in the water. Lessons begin on the sand, with you lying on your stomach and then standing on the board to get used to the feeling. One small step builds on another, all preparing you for something else.

2. Make Your First Step Stand Alone

In *The ONE Thing,* Gary Keller and Jay Papasan introduce something called the Focusing Question: "What's the ONE

Thing I can do such that by doing it everything else will be easier or unnecessary?"²

Build your routine on a single action that makes all the following actions easier or unnecessary, and you'll feel prepared even when the routine gets cut short. In fact, you might not need ten or twenty steps when the first one does such a good job.

If you're wanting to be more productive when you sit down at your desk to work, there are likely a dozen things that can help you do that, but maybe playing a certain kind of music makes the lack of a to-do list or hot coffee motivating enough to get going.

Explore what gives you the biggest bang for your buck, and begin your routine with that one step.

3. Remember Where You're Going

Once lists and steps enter the conversation, it's easy to forget they're not the point. Being prepared for something that matters is the point.

Routines aren't meant to control your environment or box you into a *Groundhog Day** life, where the same day is set to repeat over and over again. They're intended to remind you of what you value before life gets so busy that you forget.

Shall we practice building some routines together? Let's start with a morning routine since most of us have one.

A MORNING ROUTINE

What matters in the morning? What energy do you want to carry in your body and mind, even when the circumstances aren't ideal? Don't overthink it; just name it.

---

*My husband's longtime celebrity crush is Andie MacDowell because of this movie, and I find this excessively endearing.

Now, start small by choosing one thing to get you there, and remember where you're going.

My morning *attitude* matters because it often affects my entire day. If I start out grumpy, discontent, or isolated, I usually stay that way. Once a day gets rolling with making lunches, meeting deadlines, and shopping for groceries, I struggle to find the energy to get back to myself. Plus, when my bad attitude disconnects me from what matters, I tend to see ordinary situations as enormous, insurmountable obstacles.

On days with positive morning energy, putting out fires feels like snuffing out candles. On days with negative morning energy, I'm fighting forest fires with a dollar-store water gun.

Starting the day remembering what matters is essential for a well-lived day.

My one thing that makes everything else feel easier or unnecessary is *choosing what to think about that day.* I've already mentioned my caffeinated-squirrel brain, which always seems to be thinking about countless things at once. My mental energy is distributed among dinner plans, book outlines, how a particular friend is doing, and how the lady at the checkout line might think I'm a garbage mother because I joked about leaving my kids in the parking lot.

So many thoughts.

Too many thoughts.

Some matter, many do *not,* and this is why I'm already tired before the sun even comes up.

For the last year or so, I've started my day by choosing what I'm allowed to think about. That might sound intense, but it's necessary for my mental health. I take stock of my thoughts and remove what doesn't matter: the negative podcast review out of a thousand positive ones, how my skin looks older today compared to yesterday, and what to serve at Thanksgiving dinner when it's still August and *it's not time yet, Kendra.* I also think through what does matter and prioritize those things. Yes, choosing what music I'll play during our church's women's retreat next month is important but not as urgent as practicing what I'm supposed to play at church this Sunday. I simply choose what matters *and* what matters most that day. Other thoughts will eventually get their turn.

By building my morning routine on this practice of remembering what matters, both on my task list and in my soul, I'm better equipped to meet the day, no matter the shape it takes.

MY ROUTINE FOR WHEN
I FEEL STUCK IN MY WORK

I learned quickly that I need breaks. Some people can write or consult or sell for hours on end, but my brain can't handle long stretches.

I have an hourglass in my office that lasts around forty minutes. When I sit at my desk, I turn the hourglass, work until it empties, and then check my phone for a couple of minutes. Normally, Instagram and the constant thought of What if somebody texts something urgent? *are killers to my focus, but I know I can go forty minutes without picking up my phone.*

After the phone check, I turn the hourglass again, work until it empties, and then leave my office and do some-

Over time, I've added other elements—reading, stretching, drinking hot coffee in silence—but by starting with my one thing, I'm prepared for what's coming, even if an early riser cuts my routine short.

A ROUTINE TO START WORK

You and I likely have different types of work, but we both need a path to prepare for it. How you prepare for it is up to you, but if you create a routine not around what you *do* but what you *ask,* you'll find an easier path into your work.

Every time you begin your work, ask yourself, *What matters*

thing active, creative, or relational for five or ten minutes. Sometimes I hit the jackpot and get to do all three.

My office is in a church, and I work with people who were friends before they were office mates. Usually during those ten minutes, I walk laps around the sanctuary (active), maybe listen to some voice messages from friends while I walk (relational), play the piano (creative), or chat with a friend on my walk back (relational again).

Those ten minutes give me exactly what I need to do increasingly better work for the next two turns of the hourglass.

Maybe the start of your work isn't where you need a routine. Maybe it's the middle.

about my work? What energy do I want to carry in my body and my mind as I enter into it, even when the circumstances aren't ideal? Then choose the one thing that will have an impact in preparing you for work even if nothing else happens.

My routine to start work has gone through many evolutions over the years, mostly because my work has too. The way I begin my work depends on what my work is. The routine is different when I'm brainstorming podcast episodes on my couch than when I'm writing this book at my desk in my office, and that's why I love Lazy Geniusing a routine.

The point isn't to have the same detailed routine every day you work. Instead, ask yourself what matters about your work today, start small with the one thing that can prepare you best for that work, and then do it. *That's* your routine. What you choose might be helpful for months, or it might be best for today alone. The power of a work routine comes from asking the questions and following through on what you need today, not necessarily from sitting in the same place and using the same pen.

I already mentioned how music might set the stage for getting into work mode, and that's definitely true for my work. Sometimes my get-into-work-mode routine involves pouring myself a second cup of coffee, reflecting on what I'm doing, or lighting a candle, but the one thing I always start with is music.

> **The power of a work routine comes from asking the questions and following through on what you need today, not necessarily from sitting in the same place and using the same pen.**

Different music fits different tasks. Brainstorming in front of a whiteboard needs upbeat Taylor Swift. Deep writing work needs moody piano from Ólafur Arnalds. Menial but necessary computer tasks need Penny & Sparrow. Again, the specific music isn't routine. The power of music as it relates to what I'm doing that day *is*, and therefore, I'll always start with it.

Build a routine based on what you need, remember what matters about your work, and start with the one thing that will have the biggest impact.

AN EVENING ROUTINE

What matters about your evenings? What energy do you need to nurture?

Some days, your evening routine prepares you to look forward to tomorrow. Other times, it helps you remember today.

As long as you start small and remember what you're preparing for, your evening routine will take the shape you need it to. Most evenings will likely look the same, but by approaching your routine like a Lazy Genius, you have the freedom to prepare for what matters to you today.

For years, the only step in my evening routine was resetting the main area of the house. I'd return toys to baskets, wipe down the kitchen counters, and put the pillows back on the couch. I'd purposely go slowly rather than rushing through it since the speed of my body often affects the speed of my brain.* This routine served its purpose by preparing me for a slower, more intentional start to the next day.

Now my evening routine includes listening to music while I reset the house and lighting candles as I go. If my husband

---

* I'm pretty sure my Patronus is a feral cat.

is done putting the boys to bed, I skip the music and talk with him instead while we tidy up together. Sometimes I even have time for a walk around the block, a delight when it's been five hours since I've been alone. Those things have little impact on preparing me for the next day, but they have an immense impact on how I feel about myself and my people in that moment.

An evening routine can prepare you for tomorrow and also remind you of what matters right now.

IGNORING WHAT EVERYONE ELSE SWEARS BY

You've probably read all the articles I have about how starting your day sweating is the best thing you can do: Supermodels do it. CEOs do it. If you're not getting up before the sun to aggressively work out, what are you doing with your life?

It's hard to choose your one thing when others are so passionate about theirs. That's why a lot of self-help books are discouraging. They tell you, "Do _____, and your life will change."

At different times in my life, I've started my morning with intense cardio, with a giant glass of lemon water, with fifteen minutes of journaling, and with categorizing my to-do list, all because someone else swore that it was the best way to start my day.

• • •

Build your routines slowly, please. I know I'm a broken record at this point, but if you build them too big and too fast, they will always let you down. The ideal is to have this amazing routine up and running tomorrow, but when it fails and you're still struggling to find your way months later, you'll be further behind than you would have been if you'd done one thing every day and never added anything else.

But here's the thing: you get to choose the best way to start your day.

I like quiet mornings and not being sweaty, so why would I do intense cardio?

I like coffee and feel sick when water hits my empty stomach, so why would I drink lemon water?

I get frustrated that my brain works faster than my pen, so why would I journal?

I can trick myself into making my to-do list the most important thing instead of paying attention to the try-hard narrative running through my brain, so why would I color-code and categorize?

If an activity doesn't prepare you for what matters to you, it's just noise.

You're allowed to ignore something if it doesn't matter to you, and others are allowed to do something different from what you do if it matters to them.

TO RECAP

- The routine itself isn't what matters. It's simply an on-ramp to help prepare you for what does.
- When building a routine, start small, do one thing that has a major impact, and never forget where you're going.
- Create a routine for any task or time of day, but begin with what matters to you, not with the steps to get there.

— ONE SMALL STEP —

Evaluate your mornings through a Lazy Genius lens and see if you're preparing for the right thing. If not, choose one small step to move you in that direction and then do it.

Routines are beautifully helpful in leading you where you want to go, but what if you're not the only person who lives in your house? How can you get other people on board with this Lazy Genius Way? The next chapter is your answer: house rules.

SET HOUSE RULES

Lazy Genius Principle #6

Before my husband and I got married, we dated like people do, but we hit the intensity *hard*. On our first date, he came to my sister's wedding and met my entire extended family. On our second date, we talked about marriage—as in, *to each other*. On date number three, I met his parents.

I do not recommend this, by the way.

Kaz* is Japanese, and on that first trip to his parents' house, he told me it's a cultural thing to take off your shoes before going inside. When I walked in the door, it was like when kids play that the floor is lava, because I refused to let a sliver of leather hit the carpet before the boots came off.

Maybe you haven't dated a Japanese guy with parents who don't wear shoes in the house, but you've likely been inside a house that had a rule you didn't know about until you broke it. It's not fun, is it?

I've been in homes where I felt on guard, paying attention to every little thing so I didn't offend my hosts. Maybe you've visited someone's home for the first time and thought as you left, *Well, they're never inviting me back.*

* Rhymes with *Oz*, not *jazz*.

When you go full genius about the rules for your own house, you're likely focusing on something you wish didn't affect you so much: your reputation, how impressive your interior décor is—your general insecurity about not being enough. Deep down, most people want to be free of those things. We want to be people who live authentically and are accepted for it.

The pendulum swing to the other side is a lazy approach to house rules—as in, not having any rules at all.

Lazy Genius house rules are different. You don't need to cover your couch with plastic and frantically rush for the Dust-Buster when a kid drops a cracker on the floor. That's living in protection mode, and, man, is it exhausting. But you also don't have to live in a frat house with all its questionable substances.

Lazy Genius house rules are simple choices that support what matters to you and your people. Yes, they're practical and tangible, but they're meant to lead to a home environment of connection, not protection.

I know you well enough to know which home you'll choose.

Let's explore how house rules help us connect.

CONNECTION OVER PROTECTION

We've all experienced days when the dominoes are falling fast and in the wrong direction. Somehow one choice has led to a dozen unintended ones, everything is falling apart, and we don't know where it all went wrong.

Your reaction in these moments is usually to protect something: the house you just cleaned, the shirt you just washed that somehow is immediately muddy, or your own sanity. It's a natural instinct, but it doesn't usually lead you in a helpful direction.

Maybe you withdraw. You shut down, give short answers to every question, and feel like total garbage. You may also get angry. (That's me, by the way.) When the chaos doesn't stop, I blame my kids and tell them they're slobs instead of taking a breath and telling myself the truth about what really matters.

In those moments, it helps to remember that it's easier to clean up a cup of spilled milk than it is to mend a second grader's hurt feelings.

Chaos means different things to different people, but certain situations might lead you to resent the size of your home or your bank account. You might feel frustrated that your husband doesn't help out more. Or you might scroll Instagram and fall deeper into comparisons that keep the protective narrative going.

This is where Eating Chocolate While Angry usually happens for me.

Yes, I like order, but not at the expense of connecting effectively with my family or kindly with myself. This is why Lazy Genius house rules are different than, say, an arbitrary rule to always use a coaster. Your house rules help you move through your day in a way that ensures that the dominoes stay upright until you're ready to tip them in the direction you want rather than them falling backward on their own because a kid forgot to put the juice away.

Connection, not protection, is the goal.

HOW TO STOP THE FIRST DOMINO FROM FALLING

Stepping on a Lego won't turn me into a monster, but stepping on a Lego *after* I've cleaned boogers off the couch, found a permission slip that was due two weeks ago, and realized I left a gallon of milk in the van for a few hours 100 percent will.

How can you identify that first domino and keep it from falling? Start paying attention to when you protect instead of connect. What times of day do you isolate yourself or get angry on a regular basis? What does your high schooler do that makes you want to climb the wall?

Name where you currently feel enraged and protective but would rather be engaged and connected. By creating a house rule to keep that first domino from tipping, you keep the rest of the dominoes—and your connection with others—upright.

Remember that Lazy Geniuses start small. One rule at a time. Get everyone on board and see what happens.

NO HOUSE RULE FITS EVERY HOUSE

What works for me won't necessarily work for you. We all prioritize different things, we're all triggered by different emotions, and we all experience connection differently.

As I share my house rules, pay more attention to how I discovered each one than to the rule itself. It's better for you to see the process of identifying a house rule than it is to follow mine to the letter. Don't copy someone else's rule even though it might feel safer to do so. You're allowed to trust your own voice and choose what works best for you.

Now let's run through some of my house rules.

AN AFTER-SCHOOL HOUSE RULE

I've already shared about the madness that comes after school. The number of tasks that have to fit into that two-hour window between pickup and dinner is kind of stupid, and it's easy to turn into Hulk Mom in no time.

I've eliminated a lot of that angst by using the Magic Question: *What can I do now to make after school easier later?* Answer: a snack platter. But a snack platter isn't a rule. It doesn't happen every day, and it's not the only thing that keeps my dominoes from falling.

After paying attention to our afternoons for a while, I realized that the starting point for me—the first wobbling domino—was school stuff on the floor. The boys used to come home from school and immediately drop their backpacks and lunch boxes, and I would inevitably trip on them within two minutes and feel like prey in the wild. My survival instinct is highly developed.

In addition to activating my stress response, school stuff on the floor would lead to everything else ending up there. Along with their backpacks and lunch boxes, the boys would pull out their homework folders and permission slips, and everything would get lost because the floor was apparently like the Bermuda Triangle. Clutter is a magnet, and floor clutter feels way more overwhelming to me (and inviting for my kids) than clutter on a counter.

Enter the toddling little sister. Annie would see her big brother's discarded art project and assume it was hers for the taking. She's three, and anything on the floor is fair game to a three-year-old. When big brother noticed her playing with his art project, he'd scream and sob because his heart was broken, which would cause the other brother to scream and sob because he doesn't know how to process other people's displays of emotion. Meanwhile, Annie would rip the art project in half, and I would be too late to stop her, having tripped on yet another backpack.

You think I'm kidding, but this was an average afternoon. Poor Kaz would walk into an emotional knife fight every time he got home from work.

Guess what our after-school house rule is?

School stuff on the counter! School stuff on the counter!

I have to say it multiple times every single day as we walk in because they still forget, but being a singsongy nag is better than the previously described alternative.

Our house rule has changed our afternoons entirely. The mess is contained. The homework and permission slips don't get lost. I don't stub my toes anymore. Annie can't reach the counter yet, so she can't torment her brothers by taking their stuff. And Mama doesn't turn into a terrifying monster who gets mad over stupid things. Instead, I can better connect with my kids after school.

Our after-school house rule stops that first domino from falling, and afternoons are more peaceful. Not *completely* peaceful because that's impossible, but we're more likely to still enjoy one another by dinnertime thanks to one simple house rule.

A KITCHEN-COUNTER HOUSE RULE

Every design book and HGTV show says that the kitchen is the heart of the home, which might be why you often feel like you're in low-grade cardiac arrest. You have to cook all the food there, it's likely full of nonfood things like mail or bags of clothes you need to take to the consignment store, and it's the place that gets dirty the quickest because *they're seriously eating again*?

If you feel overwhelmed by the clutter in your kitchen and

feel like you can never stay on top of it, there's a good chance you let that narrative knock down a line of dominoes.

You get frustrated that no one else cares about things being clean, and you withdraw.

You find your favorite pen on the counter in a glob of peanut butter because you live with actual animals, and you get mad.

You tell yourself it's all your fault because you're a lousy housekeeper and can't do anything right, and you verbally flay everyone else.

It sounds dramatic, but that doesn't make it less true. Unimportant things suddenly feel excessively important, and you don't know why you're feeling all these emotions over a messy kitchen.

House rules aren't permission to ignore these feelings or maintain control over your kitchen and your life; that's protective. Instead, a house rule is a tool to support what matters and keep you from going too far down a road you don't like to travel.

If that road starts with frustration over a messy kitchen, consider this house rule: *The kitchen counter isn't storage.*

If you think of your kitchen counter as another cabinet or drawer, you'll put anything on it and leave it there for an eternity: a stack of mail thrown on top of the fruit bowl; a corkscrew sitting next to the dish soap; library books lying way too close to the sink.

Clutter is a magnet, so the more stuff you put on your kitchen counter, the worse it gets. And the worse your attitude gets too. Maybe you're more Zen than I am, but I have a hard time focusing on connection when I'm grumpy and annoyed. It's *possible,* but it's hard.

Use your kitchen, but make it work for you. A house rule like this isn't meant to make your kitchen look like a magazine shoot or part of a house that's on the market. *Live.* But if you find that your kitchen isn't working as well as you'd like, maybe messy counters are the culprit, and a house rule can help.

Look at your kitchen counters and notice what *could* go somewhere else. Don't commit yet; just look. The bowl of bananas and oranges is nice on the counter; the plastic bag full of plastic bags is not. The jar of spatulas and tongs makes sense next to your stove; a stack of magazines does not. The pepper grinder is perfect on the counter, but it's weird if you have to reach over a bottle of Pepto-Bismol to get to it, which has *never* happened to me.*

Maybe you feel lighter with the reminder that your counters are meant to serve you in your kitchen rather than serve as an open-air junk drawer. As you enjoy the usefulness of your kitchen and the spaciousness of your counters, you also might feel a little more space in your soul. Then this afternoon when your daughter sits down at the counter to make a beaded bracelet while you prepare dinner, you won't get annoyed with her for contributing to a mess you're overwhelmed by already.

Instead, you now have an easier path to connection.

A CLOSET HOUSE RULE

This one is more for me than for my family, but it's helpful all the same.

One of the areas where I feel the most protective is my body. As previously stated, I have a cargo hold of baggage about how I should look, and what I wear is an integral part of dealing with that.

---

* It's actually super happened to me. That would've been an unfortunate pot of soup.

If I feel like myself in my clothes, it's easier for me to feel like myself in the room. I can connect with people instead of protecting myself by hiding or apologizing for the space I take up, both literally and figuratively.

For years, though, I didn't trust my opinion of how I looked in what I wore, so I always wanted a second opinion. Asking your girlfriend what she thinks of your new pants is not bad. In many ways, it's vulnerable and good. You're putting yourself out there in a text or a fitting room and letting someone look at you. For most women, that's a triumph in itself.

My problem was that I trusted someone else's opinion over my own, so I bought what my friend, my mom, and *Real Simple* told me to buy. If I really liked a sweater but someone else didn't, I wouldn't buy it. If someone else said I looked "so cute" in a dress, I'd buy it even though I felt like an overly decorated cupcake. Cupcake dresses are great, but I prefer black and denim and the occasional stripe. I basically feel like myself when I dress like Steve Jobs.

Consequently, I had a closet full of clothes I never wore. Were my friends wrong when they told me that certain clothes were flattering? Not at all, but only I know what I'll actually wear. If I wear something I'm not comfortable in, I become self-conscious and hyperaware of how I look rather than aware of the person I'm talking to.

A closet full of clothes chosen by someone else leads me to protection, not connection.

You guessed it. I now have a closet house rule: *Don't buy clothes that someone else says I should buy.*

Is that a universal house rule for every person who goes shopping? Absolutely not. But it's one that I need in order to stop that first domino from falling.

HOUSE RULES THAT ARE
LESS EMOTIONALLY FRAUGHT

Maybe I've channeled too much Eeyore energy to start us off, so let's lighten the mood a little. Yes, house rules help you keep the first domino from falling, but they don't necessarily have to relate to therapy-level insecurities.

You're simply staying focused on what matters, and some things that matter are super simple.

A House Rule for Reading

I love to read, but I lose momentum easily. In order to maintain momentum in reading, I have a house rule: *Start a new book within twenty-four hours of finishing the last one.*

If you like to process what you've read and sit with it for a while, this house rule is the opposite of what you want. But I'm not that kind of reader. My favorite books are dystopian novels with a troubled heroine, a patriarchal society that needs to crumble, an unrequited love between the heroine and someone within that patriarchal society, and some magic or planetary weapons thrown in for good measure. Those books don't typically have the kinds of messages I'd like to contemplate for hours while looking out a window.

I've learned that if I don't start a new book within a day of finishing the last one, I lose reading momentum. Since I love books and spend more money on them than I do on anything else, I want to cultivate habits that support this activity I love, this thing that *matters*.

I have a bookshelf full of books I'm excited to read, a Kindle Paperwhite in my purse, and a system to quickly and easily keep track of what I've read, but I personally need a house rule to tip over my first domino.

A House Rule for Phones at the Table

I feel like this one exists in a lot of homes. It doesn't in ours because our kids don't have phones yet and because part of our dinner rhythm is connecting with grandparents through FaceTime.

That said, a house rule of no phones at the table comes from a desire for connection.

Phones at the table might tip that first domino, resulting in a distracted dinner with no one paying attention to anyone else and you feeling angry at everyone for not talking or staying silent and berating yourself for failing as a parent.

(Okay, maybe this one skews toward therapy level too.)

Phones aren't evil, but if they're a distraction from what matters—like conversation around the table—consider a house rule that keeps the first domino from falling.

A House Rule for Cleaning Up

Messes aren't bad. In fact, messes are a sign of life, but multiple messes piled on top of one another can sometimes lead to clutter and to feelings of being overwhelmed and frustrated.

To keep our messes as intentional as we can, my family has a house rule for cleaning up: *Clean up one mess before starting a new one.*

I clean up the dinner mess before I bake a cake. My kids need to clean up the markers from their afternoon art project before they build a Hot Wheels track across the living room floor. As a family, we put away the laundry before setting up an *American Ninja Warrior* course made of couch pillows.

It's a simple house rule focused on what matters—beautiful messes that lead to connection.

A House Rule for Finding Your Keys

You don't like feeling rushed. You don't like being late.

If the line of dominoes falls because you keep losing your keys or your high schooler accidentally leaves them in the pocket of his jeans *that he's currently wearing in a place that's not your home,* create a house rule: *Keys go in this basket and nowhere else.*

Everyone follows it, everyone knows where to find the keys, and the first domino of looking for them doesn't tip over other dominoes of frustration and thoughts that your kid is irresponsible.

LOOKING FOR HOUSE RULES

What line of dominoes do you want to stop from falling? What habits do you have that distract you from what matters?

Start paying attention to where you lose it or where you forget about connection, and then backtrack. Once you get to a potential first domino, try a house rule.

I will say again that this isn't about control. We're not trying to become an army of Zen lady robots. Messes happen. Emotional breakdowns occur. Dominoes fall, and we apologize to our people when they do.

But rather than chalking these occurrences up to "that's just the way I am," we can choose house rules that help us grow and become kinder humans. They give us practical ways to identify when we're becoming versions of ourselves that we don't enjoy so much, and they help us stay focused on what matters.

Look for places to use them, invite your family to use them, and see how much smoother life feels.

TO RECAP

- House rules are about connection, not protection. They keep the first domino from tipping and knocking over a lot more.
- No house rule fits every house. Choose what works best for yours.
- The goal isn't to maintain control but to be in a better headspace to engage with what matters—namely, your people.

— ONE SMALL STEP —

Is there a fight your family has on a regular basis? Have a casual conversation together and brainstorm ideas for one simple house rule that could keep that frustration from escalating to a fight. Creating house rules isn't all on you. In fact, doing it together as a team is one of the best parts of being a family.

There is one house rule that deserves its own chapter: *Put everything in its place.*

Let's go.

PUT EVERYTHING IN ITS PLACE

Lazy Genius Principle #7

I secretly dream of living in a tiny house. A bathtub that's also a cutting board? A closet that doubles as a refrigerator? Every single item being either white or pine and amazing?

Sign me up. Kind of.

Really, what I want is simplicity.

The emotional appeal of a tiny house or living in a van, for me, is the lack of clutter. You can see everything you have, you know where to look when something is lost, and you lean into the limits a small space imposes.

Even though a tiny house makes zero sense for us, I'm still tempted by its genius approach. I think I need to start over from absolute scratch and live with very little if I want to have any sort of handle on my stuff.*

When I realize I can't in good conscience sell everything so I never again have to clean out my closets, I might decide to go lazy and let entropy take its course. No rules, to each his own, and so what if we end up on *Hoarders*?

Even though all genius or all lazy could get my family a gig on

---

* This is not true of everyone who chooses to live in a tiny house. But it would be for me.

reality television, it's not a great long-term plan. You and I both need a way to approach our stuff, and luckily, we have one.

THE TRUTH ABOUT YOUR SPACE

Regardless of how much you have, this is your Lazy Genius principle to live by: put everything in its place. Which means everything *needs* a place.

If you look at your house as finite (which it is) and the storage systems inside its walls as finite (which they are), the limits are built in. You have only so many places to put your stuff.

The likely reason you get overwhelmed by your home is that it acts as a giant junk drawer. I don't mean your stuff is junk, but you store it like it is.

When your stuff is in random stacks and piles and crammed in a variety of baskets, you're not giving it a real place where you can find it again.

Nice to meet you, clutter.

Your reaction to clutter is probably like mine—burn it all down. You have too much stuff, and you're ready to get rid of every last item. But clutter doesn't necessarily mean you have too much stuff. It means your stuff doesn't have a place. When you put everything in its place and live within the space limits of your home, your home will be at peace and hold what matters most.

You don't have to become a minimalist; just put your stuff away.

> **Clutter doesn't necessarily mean you have too much stuff. It means your stuff doesn't have a place. When you put everything in its place and live within the space limits of your home, your home will be at peace and hold what matters most.**

MAKING SPACE FOR WHAT MATTERS

I have several bookshelves because I have several hundred books. I love books and reading with my whole heart, so making space for them matters to me. This is the key to putting everything in its place. Your home is meant to hold what matters to you and your family. If something doesn't matter, it's taking space from something that does.

If I style my bookshelves with more than books, like I've seen in all the beautiful magazine spreads, it's pretty but useless. The trinkets and vases take space from my actual books, which matter to me far more than a styled bookshelf does.

If you're like me and love books, maybe the answer to your storage problems isn't another bookshelf but instead clearing out stuff that matters less than your books do. Embrace what matters and ditch what doesn't.

As you put everything in its place within the natural limits of your home, you'll see what doesn't belong simply because it doesn't have a place to land.

Make space for what matters, and you'll see more clearly what doesn't.

THE PROBLEM WITH GIANT TRASH BAG PURGES

Whenever someone reminds me how simple and intentional my space *could be,* my instinct is to grab a roll of those enormous black trash bags and throw everything away. I've driven through the donation drop-off area at the thrift store down the street more times than I can count.

I get it. Starting over, preferably without arson, is tempting. You want to clear your schedule and toss it all, but that's no more than a Band-Aid.

Like many big systems, a trash bag purge will take you only so far. You might get a quick hit of clutter-free living, but somehow you'll end up right back where you were six months ago. How does that happen?

You might not need less stuff, but you definitely need better stuff *habits*.

Focus on small, daily habits for your stuff, and your house will feel more organized and inviting without your even realizing how you got there.

You in? Let's talk about stuff habits.

STUFF HABIT #1: PUT EVERYTHING IN ITS PLACE AS SOON AS YOU CAN

Stuff is a magnet. I swear, one piece of mail on the counter sprouts into the Leaning Tower of Pizza Hut Coupons in five minutes. Your stuff gathers without your even realizing it, and if you don't regularly put everything in its place, you'll reach for the trash bags or matches again, neither of which is the solution we're going for here.

Put everything in its place as soon as you're able, and you neutralize the magnetization of clutter. Tipping over that first domino makes your entire house function in a way that leaves room for what matters.

Start small and start early. For example, after you make your coffee in the morning, put away the creamer, and put the spoon in the sink or dishwasher. Rinse out the coffeepot when you pour your final cup. Encourage your kids to put away the cereal after they pour it rather than waiting until everyone is scrambling out the door or, worse, hours later when you're cleaning up breakfast in order to make dinner. Put the mail in the basket when you walk in the door. Unpack the suitcases as soon as you come home from vacation.

I am not into the perfect robot life anymore, but this rule might sound alarmingly similar to that. However, the point of putting things away isn't to have a perfect house or to be a person who has it all together. The point is to keep your stuff from growing like a fungus, so you don't become discontent.

Putting your stuff away helps you feel gratitude for what you have instead of frustrated by how much space it takes up.

STUFF HABIT #2: KNOW WHERE SOMETHING WILL GO BEFORE YOU BRING IT HOME

Every new item you bring through your door—groceries, clothes, trinkets, storage baskets—needs a place to go.

When you're at the store and thinking about buying something, usually the consideration is whether it's worth the price or if you can even afford it. We love a deal, and we love the zing of new things, especially when they're on sale.

What if, instead, you asked yourself where you'll put it. And "I'll find a place" is not an acceptable answer.

Can you visualize where it'll go in your pantry or closet? Will you have to cram it in to make it fit? Are you willing to make a fixed decision that this item will serve you and your home well?

Asking yourself these kinds of questions *before* making a purchase is an incredibly effective stuff habit. I'm all for getting fun, new things, but do it only if those items matter to you and have defined places in your home. Otherwise, you're contributing to the clutter.

STUFF HABIT #3: THROW AWAY TRASH

I'm not being patronizing. I ignore so much trash, and you might too.

When I think of trash, I think of the obvious, marginally gross things—tissues, dirty diapers, coffee grounds. But trash is also the broken toy you keep putting back in the toy box, the remote control that's still on the coffee table even though it's the one from two televisions ago, the hair clip that won't snap closed anymore.

The more something stays in our environment, the more we forget it's there, and this is decidedly true for stuff that's turned to trash. Don't let it hang around and add clutter to your home, especially since its magnetic powers are terrifying. Put trash in its place by *throwing it away*. This seems obvious, but it's usually the most obvious things we forget.

STUFF HABIT #4: PUT AWAY ONE THING A DAY

Certain areas in your home are so crammed with random stuff that they feel insurmountable.

You know where I'm talking about because we all have at least one space like this. It's the kitchen counter, the junk drawer, the bedroom dresser, the hall closet. Often, it's too annoying to put all those random items away or, worse, to find places for them if they're homeless. Most of us have an area where those wayward items hang out until we have time to deal with them.

Which we never do.

Then they become magnetic and multiply, and you start googling tiny houses again.

Instead, choose the smallest, most manageable of those areas where stuff goes to die, and put away one thing a day.

Just one.

It feels insignificant, but you're accomplishing two important things. One, you're slowly putting everything in its place, and slow is better than nothing. Two, you're cultivating the habit of putting everything in its place, which will serve you for a lifetime.

STUFF HABIT #5: PRACTICE A TINY WEEKLY PURGE

No matter how organized you are, every area of your home needs the occasional purge.

It's helpful to be in the practice of removing what you no longer need and what no longer matters to leave room for what does.

If putting away one thing a day is doable and you're ready for more, try a tiny weekly purge. Pick a day of the week when you usually have a few minutes, and purge one small space.

The bigger your home, the longer your list of small spaces will be, but if you regularly address those small areas week after week, you'll be in a rhythm of purging your home of what no longer matters without making it a massive project every time you get too overwhelmed by your stuff.

Your small spaces might include a junk drawer, your son's dresser, the space under your bathroom cabinet, and the toy basket in the living room. Some spaces are bigger than others, but I encourage you to steer clear of attacking an entire room. It's too much too fast, so start small.

Remember, you're not organizing; you're only purging.

Simply pull out what you no longer need and what no longer matters. Put it in a bag or box and send it on its way.

Now you have more room for what does matter.

It's low stakes, low pressure, big results.

STUFF HABIT #6: PAY ATTENTION TO WHAT YOUR STUFF IS TELLING YOU

As you put everything in its place over and over again, you'll notice what matters and what's in the way. Your stuff will tell you if it should stick around.

Are you always moving several pairs of shoes to get to the one you want? Maybe it's time to toss those other shoes. Do you keep moving cans of coconut milk to get to the cans of chicken broth? Maybe you don't like cooking with coconut milk and need to stop buying it, even though the internet swears by it. Are you always returning the same little doodads to their basket, but you never see your daughter playing with them? It could be those toys are in the same basket as the toy she actually likes, and they're in the way of what matters to her.

Listen to what your stuff is telling you, and ditch what doesn't matter.

As you put everything in its place day after day using these stuff habits, you'll likely hear these messages more clearly.

THE MADNESS OF PUTTING AWAY TOYS

Thanks, Kendra, for all your ideas and good intentions, but what about all those trucks and teapots that belong to my animal children? I clean them up just to see them out again two minutes later!

Agreed. It's super annoying.

Let's play a game and imagine two different family room scenarios.

Scenario #1: Tidying up feels like swimming upstream. The room never stays neat, so why bother? The toys stay out and the kids seem fine. But for some reason, even though the floor and coffee table are covered in all their favorite toys, the kids are grumpy and complain that there's nothing to do.

It's because they're overwhelmed by choice and quite possibly don't even see what toys are out. The mess has become background noise because nothing is in its place.

Now you have a stuff problem *and* a whiny kid problem. No thanks.

Scenario #2: You (and your kids if you want) tidy up once a day. Maybe you reset the house at night so that when they wake up in the morning, they get to open and dump and discover all over again. Maybe you all tidy up in the middle of the day before naps so that sleepy minds aren't overwhelmed when they wake up and have fresh play.

(Band name. Fresh Play. Calling it.)

Remember *why* you put everything in its place: to make sure you have space for what matters, to cultivate contentment, and to connect.

Everything is about connection because connection is what matters most.

We clean up so a new mess can be made.

It's annoying but ultimately worth it.

DON'T GET TRICKED BY THE WRONG PURPOSE

Remember, as a Lazy Genius, you're allowed to care about what matters to you.

If a tidy house matters, tidy away.

If a clean house makes you happy, spray your eucalyptus cleaner with gusto.

But don't get tricked.

Clean doesn't make you better, and messy doesn't make you more real.

You're allowed to like order, to clean your house before people come over, and to limit what comes into your home because clutter negatively affects your inner life.

You're also allowed to live in disorder, to invite friends into your mess, and to have more than you need.

Most of us swing both ways at times.

As you practice this principle of putting everything in its place, you'll likely experience joy as a result. A tidy house feels good. Closets that aren't overflowing are a pleasure to open. Being able to see what you have is gratifying.

But none of this has anything to do with your value as a person. Don't forget that. Your house might be a reflection of your personality, but the state of it is not a reflection of your value.

TO RECAP

- Live within the limits of your space, no matter how big or small. Everyone's home is finite.
- As you put everything in its place, you'll see what doesn't belong. Keep only what matters.
- The clutter in your home could be due to having too much stuff, or it could mean you need better stuff habits.

— ONE SMALL STEP —

Go put away one thing. Then tomorrow, do it again.

Every time I talk about tidying up in the Lazy Genius online community, someone inevitably says, "I love this because now I can have people over!" We've briefly mentioned how you can do that no matter the state of your house, but what does it really mean to let people in—not just into your house but into your life?

LET PEOPLE IN

Lazy Genius Principle #8

Every year, the women in my precious tiny church go on a beach retreat together, and we always play Hot Seat. In case you're new to the game, it's pretty simple: somebody sits in the front of the room while the group asks her random questions about herself. It's a way to get to know one another and hear stories about breakups, favorite movies, and the last time somebody peed her pants.

When my friend Francie was called to the Hot Seat, she walked to the stool and said, "I don't know how to feel right now because I want to stay in the back of the room, but I also want you all to know me!" We laughed because *we got it*.

Being in relationships and letting people into our homes, let alone our personal messes, is something we simultaneously want and avoid.

We let the fear of rejection cloud the desire for connection.

Will they like me?

Will I like them?

How do I ask to hang out?

What if I'd rather be alone but also sometimes feel lonely?

How can I have someone over for dinner when I can barely feed my own family without going crazy?

Most of us ask these questions or others like them, so if you feel like the weirdo social caterpillar who hasn't yet turned into a butterfly, don't sweat it. We're all afraid of letting people in to some degree.

My personal track record is quite poor actually. *Oh, you'd like to hear details?*

Sure.

HOW TO *NOT* LET PEOPLE IN

If I had a dollar for every time a friend has said to me, "We're friends and I like you, but I don't feel like I really *know* you," I'd have, like, *six dollars*.

Maybe money isn't the best mic drop example here, but when you've had only a dozen really close friends during your adult life, six is a fairly staggering number.

I've tried to be a friend in both lazy and genius ways.

The lazy way was to act perfectly fine on my own, not care when I was passed over for an invite, and dismiss anyone's attempt to know me better. The lazy way was to disappear.

Allow me to share two enlightening and possibly embarrassing examples.

The first is from high school. I had a small group of friends who liked me just fine, but I didn't hang out with them after school or on the weekends. We ate lunch together, and they smiled at me in the hall, but I wasn't anyone's go-to. I wanted to be, but no one knew that because I acted like I was fine with the way things were.

I kept my distance from everyone else at school, hoping to make it out unscathed, not caring that no one knew my name. Apparently I succeeded, because when I gave a speech at

graduation, I could hear the murmurs of my classmates saying, "Who is that? Does she go here?"

Does she go here?

I achieved my goal, but gracious, that was depressing.

The second example is from college. My freshman year, I
lived with seven other girls. They would invite me to go home
with them for the weekend or out to parties, but since I was
afraid of being known and took the lazy approach of not caring (even though I cared deeply), I said no to every invitation
and stayed in my dorm room many nights eating Ben & Jerry's
chocolate fudge frozen yogurt and watching *I Love Lucy.*

Um, that's really sad.

Around the start of my sophomore year when being alone
got too lonely, I tried to be a friend the genius way. I obses-
sively cared about what people thought of me, I tried to get
thin (this is when my eating disorder went full throttle), and I
kept it *together.* I thought the way to be a good friend was to
be perfect, look perfect, know everyone, and be a model of
good behavior and a beacon of wisdom.

Yes, you would be correct that I didn't cultivate many deep
friendships during those years.*

Thankfully, over the last decade, my view of friendship has
shifted.

I've grown to embrace what matters in friendships—honesty,
vulnerability, and growing closer through conflict. I'm learning
to put effort into those things and cultivate relationships that
make me a better version of myself. Being loved for who I am

---

* Jess, you're my biggest regret from that time. Thanks for seeking me out even
when I shut you down. I know you remember our relationship differently, but I wish
I'd let you in back then. I had lots of chances and didn't take them. And I know you're
reading this because you're still one of my biggest cheerleaders, even from a distance. Thanks for loving my hard edges so faithfully.

and loving others the same way is a new approach to friendship for me, and I'm never going back. This way is too good.

I get that this might seem like a weird principle for being a Lazy Genius, but if you want to embrace what matters, relationships are top of the list. If you want to be a genius about anything of value in your life, you need *other people* to help you do it.

What does it look like to let people in?

WHY WE NEED ONE ANOTHER

Relationships help you understand yourself better. Conversations stimulate your beliefs about people and the world. Friends watch your kids and bring you dinner when you're overwhelmed. They ask good questions when you don't know how to feel about a big decision. They make you laugh and introduce you to *The Good Place* and Monopoly Deal.

When you let people in, you find support and camaraderie, and you and those in your community see one another in more authentic ways as time goes on.

> **We can't live well without connection and community.**

We can't live well without connection and community.

In *The Gifts of Imperfection,* my beloved Brené Brown defines love as "when we allow our most vulnerable and powerful selves to be deeply seen and known, and when we honor the spiritual connection that grows from that offering with trust, respect, kindness, and affection."[3]

Even the most introverted introvert needs to see and feel seen, to have someone to process with, to share with someone a moment to mark.

We need one another to give and receive love.

Sure, this principle isn't as shiny as the Magic Question, but do you know what you can do now to make life easier later? Begin to cultivate friendships by letting people in.

I concede that your desire for connection comes in a different size and shape than mine, but we can each, in our own way, practice this principle.

Let people into your home and your life, insecurities and all.

If you're like *cool it on the vulnerability, Kendra, I'm not ready yet,* no sweat. Let's doggy paddle first.

LET PEOPLE INTO YOUR HOME

You want to be the kind of person who has deep relationships, and you're smart enough to know it doesn't happen immediately. Friendships often begin simply over spaghetti or a pot of soup.

Start small and invite someone into your home.

Soon. Like this week if you can swing it.

You might be anti-Kendra in this moment for several reasons:

- You think the meal has to be perfect, but you know nothing about cooking.
- You have a busy schedule and want to go home at the end of the day and not talk to anyone, and I'm a nag for suggesting something different.
- You've been rejected in friendship before and feel nervous it'll happen again.

Every one of those reasons is valid, and I've *deeply* felt all three. But what if you decided just this once to not let those reasons have the final say?

DON'T YOU DARE APOLOGIZE

Listen: do not apologize. I don't mean don't apologize for hurting someone's feelings or for accidentally kicking a friend in the shin. I mean do not apologize for your house, your food, or your perceived inadequacy. I'm talking about when you see a deficiency and you want to make sure everyone else knows that you know.

"Sorry it's such a mess in here."

"Sorry it's so dark; we've been meaning to paint this room."

"Sorry for the work in progress; we've been meaning to finish this project."

"Sorry if the food isn't great; I'm not much of a cook."

NO.*

Myquillyn Smith, home guru and a friend of mine, said in her book *The Nesting Place,* "I realized that when I apologize for my home, I'm declaring to all within earshot that I'm not content. That I'm silently keeping score. That I put great importance on the appearance of my home and maybe, just maybe, I'm doing that when I visit your home too."[4]

You're likely a lot harder on yourself than you are on anyone else, but no one else knows that. If you have people over and apologize for how messy things are, whether it's true or not, you put your guests on their toes and distract from the entire point of inviting them over in the first place: connection.

You want to let people in with the hope of becoming friends, not to compare your life with theirs or with how you think your life should be.

You want to fill your home with people because people

---

* For those of you listening to the audiobook, sorry for the sudden burst of volume.

matter. Connection, conversation, laughter, good food, vulnerability—all these things matter. And because they matter, you get to decide how to be a genius about them. The simplest way is to have somebody over.

Need some ideas? Happy to help.

A Regular Dinner

Invite somebody, a couple of somebodies, or a family over for dinner.

Make the food yourself, go potluck, or hire it out to a trusty pizza establishment. As long as it's a meal eaten in your house, it counts as having somebody over for dinner.

If you have a desire to cook the meal yourself but don't have many skills or recipes in your arsenal, might I suggest my Change-Your-Life Chicken? It's easy, adaptable for any number of people, delicious, pretty, and basically foolproof. It's my legacy and will be on my gravestone, so if you haven't tried it, this is your chance.*

Swap Nights

My sister and her husband regularly swap nights with another couple who have little kids of similar age as theirs. After bedtime, the two women hang out at one house and the guys at the other. It's genius because the kids sleep in their own beds, no babysitters are needed, there's a parent available for any kid who wakes up, and connection happens. Bingo.

Weekend Family Breakfast

Family breakfast is one of my favorite ways to connect. It's especially great for families with young kids. Everybody is up at

---

* Google "Change-Your-Life Chicken" and you'll see it right away.

seven or eight anyway (or before six if you're at my house), so start early with homemade breakfast or a doughnut run.

You get to connect during the most low-pressure meal of the day, and you still have the rest of the day ahead of you. Plus, naps and bedtimes are beautifully unaffected by gathering at breakfast. Give it a try.

Dessert Nights

I have chocolate icing in my veins, so this is an obvious suggestion for people who know me. Pick up a pie or a pint or two of ice cream, and get to know somebody over sugar. If you have little kids, this is often easier than inviting someone for dinner, especially if you can invite people who either don't have kids or have ones old enough to be alone for an hour or two.

If you have little ones, put them to bed and then close out the day with conversation over cake. If you don't have little kids, offer to bring a late-night dessert to a family that does.

Lunch After Church

Shannan Martin, who is my favorite person to listen to when it comes to being a good friend and neighbor,* opens her home to whomever can come every Sunday after church.

Since she and her family do life within a few blocks of their home (school and church are both within walking distance), her circle is small but super intentional. She makes soup and sets out the bowls. Sometimes people bring stuff to add, and sometimes she grabs a few bags of chips from the pantry if the crowd gets big.

*Read her book *The Ministry of Ordinary Places* to have your heart rocked, please.

There's no apology, no pursuit of perfection, and no attempts at being put together, but there's always connection.

You can obviously do the same by inviting someone to a casual restaurant after church. Look for someone different from you: the college student, the empty nesters who always sit behind you, or the family with little kids even though you might now be an empty nester yourself.

One way or another, invite somebody for lunch.

Clean your house or not. Make the food or not. Take a shower or not.

Do what matters and focus on connection. The other stuff is secondary and requires no apology either way.

LET PEOPLE INTO YOUR EVERYDAY LIFE

Ordinary life is no joke. That's likely why you picked up this book. You want help getting out of life's grind and monotony, partly because it's hard but maybe even more because it's *lonely*.

All of us have a long list of responsibilities to manage, and most of us manage them alone. I find it incredibly tough to ask for help with everyday responsibilities or even to share their emotional weight with friends because my problems don't feel important enough. I don't want to be a bother, I don't want to sound like I'm complaining, and aren't we all supposed to know how to put our heads down and just get it done?

I'm so good at comparing miseries and dismissing mine in a flash. There are people without food, parents, soap, civil rights. Who am I to complain to a friend about my kid getting a phantom stomachache and making me miss my massage appointment? That's a true story, by the way. But it's also true that my back pain was intense, pain affects my mood, and my mood, as my fourth grader recently pointed out, can be "a little grumpy sometimes."

You think you're supposed to let people in only when things are really bad, but what about when your everyday challenges *feel* really bad? Carrying them alone is trying to be a genius about something that doesn't matter. Self-reliance doesn't matter if there's no community to go with it.

We're allowed to need one another. In fact, it's beautiful to do so, especially in the most ordinary, everyday moments.

YOU DON'T HAVE TO BE IN CRISIS TO ASK FOR HELP

I already said I'm historically bad at letting people in, and for years I practiced that by vowing to let people in only during a crisis. But who gets to determine what counts as a crisis? How do you decide when it's bad enough to let somebody into your everyday problems?

No one would fault you for needing childcare so you can be with your dad when he goes to chemotherapy, right? That feels like a legitimate crisis. But what if you're struggling with anxiety? I mean, it's mostly manageable. You can get through the day, but life requires more energy than you have to give. Even though you're struggling under the weight of a very real problem, it feels invisible and hard to justify. An afternoon alone, a listening ear, or an hour for a nap would be a gift, but nothing about being anxious feels important enough to warrant asking for help.

Or what if you're straight up tired? You've had a long stretch of difficult days, your hormones aren't helping, and you feel like making dinner will drain you of any spark you have left.

That's definitely not important enough.

Only *it is.*

Crisis is not a prerequisite for seeking community and connection.

You don't have to be fine all the time. You're allowed to struggle, to feel overwhelmed by your responsibilities. You're allowed to share the pressure you feel over where to send your kid to school. Do you feel guilty even worrying about the decision because you're choosing between a private school that most people can't afford or a charter school that hundreds of kids didn't get into? Guilt is one of many emotions that keep us from letting people in.

We're so good at putting qualifications on our struggles, and if the problems are too niche, too ordinary, too privileged, or too [fill in the blank], we don't share them. We keep people out and say everything is fine.

That's likely why six of my twelve friends didn't know me. I never let them into the regular stuff. I didn't share how nursing a baby who struggled and regularly bit my boob would shift my entire day. I didn't share that I didn't know how to tell my husband I missed him even though he was sitting right next to me on the sofa. I didn't share how I felt unfulfilled in my job even though it was great work with great people. I felt I had no right to complain.

There was no *real* crisis, in my opinion, so I kept my mouth shut. But if you and I wait for tragedy to strike before we let people in, we miss out on all the beautiful, ordinary connection. We miss out on the coffee deliveries in the middle of a hard day or the text messages or funny GIFs because a friend knows we're weary from nothing and everything and simply need a laugh.

We miss out on ordinary connection that leads to deeper relationships.

Start letting people into your everyday struggles, and don't worry about whether they're tragic enough.

Say yes when a friend asks if you need anything from Target.

Say yes when your sister offers to watch your kids, and don't immediately start thinking of how you can pay back the debt because, really, there isn't a debt at all.

Say yes when your spouse offers to clean up the kitchen tonight so you can go to bed early instead of believing you're stronger for powering through.

We're all broken, beautiful people trying to let one another in, and the everyday moments are a great place to start.

SHARE THE EYE POKES

Part of being human is doing life together. No pretense, no crisis, just the ordinary middle of your ordinary days.

Emily* and I call these eye poke moments. We share things that aren't super important but also very much are because they're real and happening to us, no matter how simple or silly. They're just eye pokes.†

The irony is that eye poke moments feel more sacred when you share them with someone who's actually been with you in crisis. Emily and I eye poked for a while, but then we also lived some real life together. We had arguments and misunder-

---

*P. Freeman.

† In hindsight, this terminology is more violent than I realized. We don't actually poke each other in the eye.

standings; we each had major career decisions to work through; we ugly-cried and shared things that felt too scary to bring into the light.

I've wept in front of people only half a dozen times in my life, and Emily has been there for at least half of them. Does that mean we talk only about serious things now? Are you *kidding*? I'm pretty sure we've spent a solid half hour on Meghan Markle's outfits alone. But those silly, everyday, ordinary conversations hold as much importance as the hard stuff does, making every conversation significant because our relationship matters to both of us.

> Deep relationships don't come from letting others into the deep stuff only; deep relationships come from a willingness to let others into *all of it*.

Deep relationships don't come from letting others into the deep stuff only; deep relationships come from a willingness to let others into *all of it*.

An interaction doesn't count less because no one bared her soul—at least in the way you might typically define it. You can bare your soul in ordinary, everyday moments too.

The soul holds space for both eye poke and crisis moments, and so can you and your people, which leads to the deep connection you long for.

WHEN THINGS WEREN'T FINE FOR ME

Writing this book has been a unique opportunity for me to let people in. This work is far from a stereotypical crisis, but it's also the hardest project I've ever undertaken. My personality isn't naturally built to withstand the long runway that is book writing. You have to write so many garbage words in order to find the good ones, and if you haven't picked up on this yet, I'm a bit of a recovering perfectionist.

I quickly saw that even though I had to write this book alone, I couldn't *carry* it alone.

As recently as an hour before I wrote this section, a friend popped her head into my office and asked, "How's the writing going?" Dozens of people have asked me that question over the last eight months, and I no longer answer, "Fine!"

"Fine" isn't true. Sure, writer's block isn't an emergency, but I'm choosing to let people into my *feeling* that it is. "Fine" keeps people out and leaves me isolated, so I've learned to answer differently:

"It's hard today."

"A bit of a slog, but I'm finding my way."

"I finally found the thread of this chapter, so I'm pumped!"

"I hit my word count goal earlier than I thought, so I'm going to treat myself and pick up Chipotle on the way home."

It felt strange to be this forthcoming at first, because who actually cares?

Turns out my people do, and the more I let them in, the more practice we get at caring for one another. Skipping the "fine" has deepened so many of my relationships in ways I never expected.

If you're in the ordinary middle of a project, a job, or even a stage of life, don't assume it's not important enough to let people in. You might have a responsibility or emotional burden that's all your own, but that doesn't mean you have to carry it alone.

It doesn't always have to be fine.

Let people in.

WHEN CONNECTION DOESN'T HAPPEN

Sometimes we don't connect with someone. The chemistry isn't there, or we don't have much in common. That's part of life and doesn't mean anything negative about the people involved. Not everyone you date is a match; the same goes for friendship.

Still, it's easy to internalize the lack of connection as a personal failure. You weren't enough for that person. You weren't cool enough or interesting enough. You were too weird or too quiet or too loud. You feel like you're what's wrong, so the impulse is to change who you are.

If after-school specials have taught us anything, it's that changing who you are to be accepted doesn't get you anywhere. Sure, you might not be flat-out rejected, but you won't be truly accepted either. If you focus on not being rejected, you'll miss out on what you're really after: connection.

Sometimes being accepted for who you are takes longer than you want and hurts while you wait, but it'll come. You'll eventually find your people when you're willing to let them in.

It's risky to be the one to reach out first, but it's worth it in the end.

TO RECAP

- It's okay if you don't come away with a lifelong friendship after inviting someone over. It's still worth it.
- Let people into your everyday life without apology.
- You don't have to be in a crisis to ask for help.
- Don't overthink connection. Just invite somebody over.

— ONE SMALL STEP —

Text someone to share an eye poke or to invite her to hang out. Maybe now?

If you're a little shaky after all that relationship talk, let's shift gears and discuss the shiny life hack of batching.

BATCH IT

Lazy Genius Principle #9

Can I claim I was once a professional baker because I had a business where I sold what I baked? We'll say yes. The Sugar Box was an endeavor where I'd create desserts inspired by a particular pop culture theme and box them up all cute and pretty. Locals would order them online and pick them up from my front porch one day a month (i.e., Sugar Box Day).

I loved it and was good at it.

I was not, however, good at numbers and eventually realized I was making two cents an hour for each box I sold. Let's just say the *Shark Tank* people would not have invested in me.

But I learned a lot in that year and a half: I became a better baker, I saw how much I came alive when I gathered people around food, and I learned to batch—first in cookies, then in life.

THE LESSON FROM BAKING A THOUSAND COOKIES IN A SINGLE DAY

On Sugar Box Day, everything had to be ready at once. And by everything, I mean several thousand individual desserts wrapped into several hundred bundles and lovingly tucked into forty to seventy boxes. They were brown paper packages tied up with string, and they were absolutely one of my favorite things.

Getting those boxes ready all at once, month after month, turned out to be a master class in batching. My first lesson came on my very first Sugar Box Day. I had forty-five orders for the *Friends* box,* so I started packing them one by one. I got a stack of one kind of cookie, put it in a bag, cut a string, tied up the bag, and put it in the box. I did the same with another stack of cookies, followed by a tower of brownies and four or five more different treats. I packed each box, one by one, and it took *forever.*

The system got better the next month. I stacked the cookies in piles of the right number, cut all the string at once, wrapped bundle after bundle, *and then* tied them together one after the other. So much faster.

Eventually, the baking itself got batched too. I'd mix the cookie doughs on the same day since they used similar ingredients and had a similar technique. Then I'd form over a thousand cookie dough balls all at once and freeze them to bake later. When later came, I'd bake all the cookies one tray after another like an actual machine.

I learned that I couldn't work with only one recipe or one Sugar Box at a time. Instead, I had to do similar tasks all at once to efficiently move the project forward.

Then I started noticing how the same could be true in my everyday life. Batching could transform more than baking.

---

*Contents included Paleontology Cookies (sugar cookie dinosaurs that said "pivot"), Joey's Chick and Duck Jam Sandwich Cookies, Phoebe's Grandmother's Chocolate Chip Cookies, Central Perk (coffee-flavored) Marshmallows, Princess Consuela Banana Hammock Banana Bread, and fudge mint brownies inspired by Phoebe's love of pot brownies. It was a Phoebe-heavy box.

HOW BATCHING WORKS

Batching is a specific kind of task done over and over before you move on to the next thing. Don't let the simplicity fool you; this little principle has power.

Think about factory assembly lines. A single person is responsible for a single task, the next person is in charge of the next task, and so on, down the line. The factory has a lot of output because one person isn't building each individual refrigerator from scratch.

It's likely you build many of your projects from scratch when instead you could batch their tasks and get them done a little quicker. Not only that, but batching gives your brain a break since you're essentially turning it on autopilot.

Now, we've already established that you're not a robot, and turning you into one is definitely not the goal of this book. But the truth is that some things are better automated.

Factories get a bad rap because nothing is handcrafted, and isn't made by hand always better? Yet if you apply that mind-set to your home, expecting everything to be done with exceptional attention, you're being a genius about everything and lazy about nothing and you will find yourself exhausted and in need of afternoon chocolate and ongoing therapy.

Not everything has to be thoughtful. Some of your work can be automated for the sake of your time and energy, leaving those valuable resources for the pursuits you *want* to be thoughtful about.

WHAT TO BATCH

How do you find jobs to batch? Look for tasks you repeat and jobs you find you need to undo.

An example of a repetitive job is making lunches for kids. You have to make three sandwiches, cut up three apples, slice three piles of carrot sticks . . . you get the idea. You might make one kid's sandwich, pack it up, cut up an apple, pack it up, slice the carrots, and pack them up—*or* you could batch the repeated tasks.

How do you find jobs to batch? Look for tasks you repeat and jobs you find you need to undo.

Spread peanut butter on three slices of bread one after the other. Next comes the jelly. Close all the sandwiches. Put them all in bags. Slice all three apples at once. Slice all the carrots at once. Bag all the fruits and vegetables at once.

Find tasks you repeat and do them at the same time.

In terms of work you might have to undo, the dishwasher is a great example. How many times have you loaded the dishwasher and then found a stack of plates and a pot that won't fit because of how the dishwasher is loaded? It could all fit, but now you have to undo what you already did.

Not if you batch first. Bring all your dishes to the dishwasher at once, and load it only when all the dishes are in front of you. Now you can load once and save time.

I'll get into more particulars with that example and many more, so let's dive in to batching.

LAUNDRY

Laundry is a batching dream. Put a couple of key batches together, and you do your laundry from start to finish in the same day. Sounds like a fantasy, right?

The struggle with laundry is that you're confronted with as

many tasks as there are items of clothing. From every shirt to every sock, each item technically has to be tended to from start to finish—sorted, washed, dried, folded or hung up, and put away. If you were to do that with each item one at a time, your anger and frustration would be on par with a Marvel Universe alien invasion. It's stupid to do laundry that way. You already know that, which is why you wash and dry in loads.

But we can batch even more than that.

Sorting and Washing

With a few exceptions, you can wash lights and darks together. I know our beautiful mothers told many a cautionary tale about mixing colors, but beyond the obvious "don't wash your favorite white T-shirt with a new pair of dark jeans," you can wash different colors together.*

So, how do you sort then, if not by color?

By where clothes end up.

Wash all the clothes that go on hangers in *your* closet in one load. Wash your toddler's clothes in another. Wash the towels together, the school uniforms together, the "anything that ends up in the same place" *together*. Now you can more quickly hang up your shirts without having to sort through your teenager's socks and your preschooler's unicorn sweatpants.

Folding

Now, listen up. If you're into this laundry batching idea, please don't ruin your momentum by dumping all the laundry together on the couch. Otherwise, you have one giant pile that has to be sorted all over again as it's folded.

---

*Stick with cold water to be safe.

Don't ruin your batches!

Washing your clothes based on where they end up is a gift, and if you're into it, you can continue batching as you fold. In loads where there are more than a few kinds of items,* you can quickly sort them into piles.

Start with the biggest items first because they're easier to spot: jeans, towels, or whatever seems obvious. Continue pulling out the biggest, most obvious items until you're left with a pile of socks or washcloths or whatever is smallest. Now you can fold in batches.

Fold all the towels at once and get into the rhythm of those motions; you don't have to search for the towels because they're in a pile right in front of you.

Pair up the socks easily because they're all in one pile.

Fold shirt after shirt and lean into those repeated actions.

Your brain will happily go into automatic as it tends to one kind of item the same way over and over again.

Putting Laundry Away

I'm not going to tell you to save steps by putting your piles away in terms of what room you hit first (although I have done that myself), but I will encourage you to put a load of laundry away right after you fold it.

You've done the work of sorting and washing based on where it ends up, so everything you folded will likely go to one room. Scoop it up and take it there before your living room gets overtaken with piles and your brain has to start processing more information than necessary.

---

*I often wash all the gross stuff on hot: underwear, socks, cleaning rags, etc. Since I don't wash much on hot, all those items get grouped together to save the planet. *You're welcome.*

Let your brain work hard on what matters, not on routine work you can easily batch.

Laundry Day

The only job I do on Laundry Day is, you guessed it, laundry. By engaging only in this job, I'm already batching. I'm doing one kind of task over and over again, automatically.

Laundry Day keeps me from having to remember when a load is done because I got distracted cleaning the bathroom. By focusing all my energy on one repetitive chore, it gets done more quickly and without having to rewash loads because I forgot about them and now the house smells like an old, wet cat.

The Stray Laundry Zone

I got tired of carrying our cloth napkins and stray socks and every other bit of random dirty laundry to the laundry room. I

IF YOU HAPPEN TO LIKE LAUNDRY

If laundry doesn't fill you with rage, you likely think all this is borderline crazy. Maybe it is, and maybe your lack of batching feels fine. You've always washed what you could when you could and folded the giant pile at the end of the day without complaint. If that's life giving, go forth and fold.

But don't assume that's the only way. If you don't hate laundry, still try batching one part of it and see if the process feels different. If it does, you might end up liking laundry even more.

realize this is a very privileged problem, but it was annoying all the same.

Now I have a Dirty Laundry Zone, a galvanized steel container I bought at a home store for ten dollars. It sits in the corner of my kitchen, and it's where we put all the dirty laundry we find in that part of the house. Rather than carrying each dirty item to the hamper, I drop it in the bucket and save my steps. When the bucket is full, I take it to the hamper. The task is batched. Hallelujah.

CLEANING THE KITCHEN

You've made dinner and possibly still have dishes out from lunch or breakfast, and cleaning feels necessary but terribly overwhelming. You have to deal with the kitchen table, the counter, and the sink, all littered with different kinds of items that need different kinds of attention before they end up in completely different places.

The reason a dirty kitchen is so stressful is because your brain cannot figure out which task to do first. Each one feels equally urgent. Man, does batching shine in a dirty kitchen.

Clearing Off Surfaces

Usually, you pick something up from the kitchen table, carry it to the dishwasher, load it, pick up a random plate that's close by, load it, and then put away the ketchup on your way to wiping up milk from under the table. You dart around like a pinball, grabbing at whatever is closest.

Instead, clear off one surface at a time and to completion. Then move on to the next area.

Clearing off in batches is a mental victory because there's

less mess for your brain to process and you feel the momentum as each surface empties.

I always start with the kitchen table. It's the farthest surface from the sink and usually the least intense. It's a quick win.

DECIDE ONCE
HOW YOU'LL BATCH CLEAN

Want a bonus tip? Decide once (remember that principle?) in what order you'll clean your surfaces. Mine is kitchen table first and kitchen island second. Then I work around the main counter from the stove side to the sink side. That's my order every single time I'm in the kitchen, and my brain loves me for it.

Putting Stuff Away

When you're cleaning your kitchen, create physical places for your batches to go; I call them zones. Zones help you go on autopilot because you know exactly where to put an item down. Not *away*, just down.

Remember the tip of batching tasks you have to undo? How many times have you played Fridge *Tetris* because you put items away as you touched them rather than putting them away all at once? Inevitably, there's a carton of eggs or a big plastic container of leftovers or some other awkwardly shaped item that needs to go in the fridge, and you can't figure out how to make everything fit.

Use batching to put everything away at once, and use zones to hold those items until you're ready.

KITCHEN ZONES

Choose areas next to all your kitchen's final destinations, and keep items together until you're ready to put them away all at once.

Examples: Fridge Zone, Pantry Zone, Dirty Dishes Zone, and Dirty Laundry Zone.

I'd say Freezer Zone, but that might not end well. Be speedy on that one.

And a Trash Zone is your trash can. You don't usually have to play Tetris *to get all the trash to fit; simply stick everything in the bin.*

Loading the Dishwasher

Do not load the dishwasher until all dirty dishes are in the Dirty Dishes Zone.

Let's make this a chant, please. Somebody print it on a tea towel.

If you wait for every dish before you start loading the dishwasher, you know what you're working with. If you don't wait, you'll be forced to play Dishwasher *Tetris* and undo a ton of work.

Batch instead.

As you clear off your surfaces, put all the dishes in the Dirty Dishes Zone. Once you have all the dishes in front of you, you can load the dishwasher in an order in which everything may actually fit on the first try.

Start with what can go only on the bottom rack (plates,

pots, big dishes), followed by what can go only on the top rack (little plastic dishes that might melt). Then fill in the gaps with what's left.*

PAPER

You thought you were drowning in laundry and dishes? Paper is a force of nature.

We all have mail and receipts by the truckload, and if you have kids, you also have artwork, school projects, permission slips, report cards, flyers about sports camp and piano lessons and birthday parties . . . stop me anytime.

Each piece of paper, like each item of clothing, has to go through a process of sorting, deciding, and storing. Every single piece.

If you tend to each piece individually as it catches your attention, you'll go crazy. Still, you can't throw everything into a giant pile and go through it only when you can no longer see the kitchen table or when your electricity gets turned off.

Batching is how you deal with *the same kinds of paper all at once,* not all the paper all at once or every piece on its own.

In the same way they helped in the kitchen, zones will help you group your papers into appropriate categories so you can deal with the same kind all at once. I'll share some examples of zones I use, but the point is to recognize what categories of paper you have and hold them in a zone until you can deal with them.

---

*I shared some of these ideas on my show, *The Lazy Genius Podcast,* and I loved getting the whiplash-y emails from people who thought I was legit insane to put this much thought into cleaning the kitchen and then promised me their life savings for giving them so much direction on how to do it more easily. Yes, I'm crazy, but I'm also right.

The Time-Sensitive Zone

Papers with obvious due dates—like bills, event invitations, and school permission slips—need a designated place away from everything else.

We both know what happens otherwise. You dump all the mail on the counter with the gas bill on top so you won't forget it. Then a kid comes home and piles a bunch of school papers there, a husband adds a car magazine, somehow a dog leash gets involved, and now you have a random mess that stresses you out.

Sorting that pile requires more energy than necessary because every item requires a different action. You can't batch a giant pile.

Instead, have a zone for time-sensitive items, and go through that stack every week or two. Pay the bills, sign the forms, text the RSVPs all at once.

I love sitting down with my Time-Sensitive Zone papers because I know what I'm getting into. And since I already sorted them into the right zone when they came in the house, dealing with those papers takes only a few minutes.

Bonus Tip #1: Put the task on your calendar or create a phone alarm to remind you to go through the pile every two weeks.

Bonus Tip #2: Put papers that need immediate attention on the fridge, on top of your purse, or in any other area that can act as a "Don't Forget About This" Zone.

The Recycling Zone

Don't waste your time with papers that do not have immediate or future implications. (I'm looking at you, catalogs.) Some papers need to go directly into the Recycling Zone.

I like to think I'm the kind of person who enjoys flipping through and buying from catalogs, but all it does is give me errands to the post office for purchases I'll inevitably return and more stuff to find a home for. No thanks.

Catalogs, coupon inserts for restaurants we never choose to go to, and all other types of junk mail need to be removed from your space right away. If you leave those papers interspersed with important ones, the sorting is more annoying and time consuming.

Instead, when you walk into the house with a stack of mail, go ahead and toss anything you know you don't need. This is decluttering more than it is batching, but it's a vital step in creating margin for what you *will* batch.

The Art Zone

I have three children who draw and paint like their lives depend on it. (I'm pretty sure for my middle kid, it does.) Their at-home projects join forces with papers from school and church, and before long, we're drowning in coloring pages and drawings of Mario.

Because we have so many projects in various stages of completion, it's silly to sort it out every day for two reasons: it takes way too long, and something that's valuable today might not be valuable tomorrow.

Enter the Art Zone.

We have a giant basket—I'm talking a set of newborn quintuplets could fit in this thing—where all the art paper goes. Every Sunday school coloring page, every piece of scrap paper, every completed masterpiece goes in this basket.

When the basket is full, and not one second before, I sort through it. The process takes maybe twenty minutes. I put the papers into categories: keep, trash, and can be used again. If my keep pile contains twenty drawings of the *Mona Lisa,* I can easily see which three I want to keep. If I had to decide what to keep every day, I might keep all twenty versions without realizing my kid was drawing the same thing over and over again.*

The keepers then go into a plastic bin full of beloved artwork, and when that bin is full (which it still isn't after nine years), I'll figure out what to do with it. The papers we can use again go back into the art closet, and everything else goes in the recycling bin.

I realize the irony of suggesting one giant dumping ground for artwork when I told you to do the exact opposite with your mail. But sorting kids' art is a different task than paying bills. You don't need to see all the mail to know what to do with a bank statement. You do need to see all the art to know what's worth keeping and what was simply fun during the process.

Some papers are best handled often, like bills, and some are best handled as little as possible, like art projects. No matter your frequency in tending to these papers, have a zone to hold them until you're ready.

The Future Zone

You tear pages out of magazines. You have a handwritten recipe for the best breakfast casserole ever because you begged your coworker for it after he brought this dish to a staff meeting. We have lots of papers that are fun for the future but don't always have a natural home. Solution? Create a Future Zone.

Put all those random clippings and scribblings in one place and then deal with them at one time. Put the recipes into a spreadsheet, snap photos of the inspiring rooms and

*This number is not hyperbole. My middle son has drawn probably over a hundred versions of the *Mona Lisa* in his seventh year of life.

put them on a Pinterest board, or add everything to Evernote. It doesn't matter so much what you do with the papers; what matters is that you do it all at once *in a batch*.

FOOD

Choosing, prepping, and cooking food is where batching really shines. Since you eat multiple times a day, streamlining the process by doing certain tasks all at once will make your life much easier. Let's run through some potential ways.

Meal Planning

Meal planning itself is a form of batching. You're doing one task—deciding what's for dinner—all at once, whether it's for a few days, a week, a month, or whatever interval makes you happy. By making that choice at one time, you leave space for other choices later.

I also make meal planning easier by combining it with the principle of deciding once. Rather than choosing my meals from an endless number of sources, I often limit myself to one cookbook and from a list of what I call Brainless Crowd-Pleasers. These dinners are easy for me or my husband to make and are generally pleasing to my family. I decide once to eat from that one cookbook and that one list for the next month. In this way, I've batched the decision-making of meal planning.

Meal Prep

If you create a meal plan and notice two recipes that use the same ingredient—diced onions, for example—then dice onions for both recipes at once. You're already doing the task; don't make things difficult by doing it more often than you have to.

You don't have to create a meal plan, though, to batch your prepping. If you come home with several packages of chicken you got on sale, don't stick them in the freezer to waste away in a land of freezer burn and unrealized potential. Batch prep the chicken.

Season all the chicken with salt, because no matter how you use it, it'll need to come out of the package and be seasoned. You can then pack it up in individual freezer bags to make dinner easier later (hello, Magic Question), or you can go even further by cutting the chicken into pieces, portioning it into bags, and filling those bags with one big batch of homemade stir-fry marinade or a store-bought variety you love.

If you have a prep task that you'll need to do more than once but *can* do it all now, batch it.

Putting Away Groceries

After a big grocery run, the tendency is to unpack the bags and put away whatever you pull out first. However, constantly shuffling items around to make room for new ones can get frustrating.

Instead, unload your groceries into zones and then put them away all at once—Fridge Zone, Freezer Zone (probably a good idea to do that one first), Pantry Zone, and so on.

I love putting groceries away in batches as a family. It's easy to trip over one another when several people are trying to put a can in the same place. With zones, one family member tackles one zone and doesn't get in the way of anyone else.

If you want to take your grocery batching to the next level, get a head start by packing your groceries in batches when you buy them. Fridge stuff in this bag, freezer stuff in that bag . . . and then come home and put it all away in batches without even having to think about it.

BATCHING SCHOOL VALENTINES

If you didn't yet think I was nuts, buckle up.

For the little class cards, don't go start to finish on every single one; do the individual tasks one at a time.

First, tear apart all those poorly perforated cards at once. Then write all the classmates' names in the "to" area at once so you can go straight down the list and not lose your place.* Next, write your kid's name because that one is easy (except when you're speaking to her; then all bets are off). Finish up by stuffing all the cards into envelopes.

I've done the process both ways, and I promise batching goes faster and uses less brain power. Autopilot is a beautiful thing for projects that don't really matter so much.

DON'T DO IT IF IT DOESN'T HELP

Batch only if it makes your life easier.

If you like looking through your kids' projects every day or want to put your groceries away however you want to, *oh my goodness, do it.* The point of batching, and any of these principles, is to make your life easier where it doesn't matter and give you more energy and time where it does.

If batching stresses you out, don't do it. It's worth it only if it helps.

* Or forget a kid. That's never happened to me. Nope. Not once. (Yes. Yes, it has.)

TO RECAP

- Batching is doing the same kind of task all at once.
- Going into autopilot while batching doesn't make you a robot but instead leaves time for what matters.
- Look for tasks you repeat often or have to undo, and see if batching can help.

— ONE SMALL STEP —

Clean your kitchen tonight using zones, and see if it speeds up the process.

Batching is a great little hack for your home, but life hacks help only when you know what parts of your life are essential. Otherwise, you're hacking stuff that doesn't matter.

Let's essentialize next.

ESSENTIALIZE

Lazy Genius Principle #10

As I'm writing these words, it's the middle of Lent, and I have given up nonwork Instagram for this short season. When the idea initially came to mind, I quickly dismissed it. It seems to me the overarching narrative is that Instagram is either all good or all bad. Either you're lazy and let it completely run your life and hijack your brain, or you're a genius because you delete it from your phone and never engage in it. I personally don't have that binary view, but I wondered if my decision to give it up for Lent would put me in the "Instagram is bad" camp.

I read Greg McKeown's book *Essentialism* every year, so his concept of choosing and ignoring with intention has become part of my marrow. As I thought about Instagram, I knew all-or-nothing thinking would be unnecessary but that essentialism would be integral. I'm on the app a lot for my job, but I had grown lazy about monitoring how often—and even more importantly *for what purposes*—I was using it.

I had forgotten what mattered.

During these last few weeks of Lent, I've remembered.

I miss seeing what my real friends put into the world. I miss laughing at Comments by Celebs. I miss James McAvoy going live from a Scottish mountaintop. Engaging in the lives of my friends, laughing, and looking at James all matter to me.*

What doesn't matter? Ads that make me buy stuff I think I need but don't, accounts I follow because they're pretty but that often lead me to comparison instead of joy, and scrolling when I'm bored. I don't miss those a single bit.

If it isn't essential, it's just noise.

Guess what will happen once Lent is over?

I'm going to essentialize Instagram.

Now that I've identified what matters, I can unfollow or mute accounts that don't support those things. No more feeds that lead me down paths of comparison, judgment, or wasted time.

If it isn't essential, it's just noise.

WHY ESSENTIALIZING MATTERS

If you want to embrace what matters and ditch what doesn't, you need to *know* what matters.

This is true not only for the life purpose statement on a canvas over your couch but also for what's in your drawers and purse and on your calendar.

When you fill your life with things that are not essential to what matters, you unintentionally add noise, and managing noise is part of why you're tired.

Naming what matters shows you what you need to support it.

Naming what matters shows you what's *essential*.

When you fill your life with things that are not essential to what matters, you unintention-

* My husband is aware of how much I love James McAvoy. We're cool.

ally add noise, and managing noise is part of why you're tired.

Did you ever play the game MASH as a kid? It was a game that predicted where you'd live (MASH stood for mansion, apartment, shack, and house), who you'd marry (because what's life to a twelve-year-old girl without a future husband?), what job you'd have, and how many kids would inevitably end your career days for good.*

We think that life is made up of big decisions, that where you live is more important than *how you live there day to day*. Instead, remember the importance of starting small. The small choices we make over and over every single day contribute more to a meaningful life than the big decisions do.

> **We think that life is made up of big decisions, that where you live is more important than *how you live there day to day*.**

The more you choose what's essential and intentionally support what matters, the less noise you have to manage and the more energy you have for a fulfilling life.

ADDITION BY SUBTRACTION

If you're like me, you probably seek out fulfillment by adding things to your life.

You feel dissatisfied choosing what to wear, so you buy more clothes. You feel overscheduled in your job, so you add more stress relievers to your calendar to compensate. You feel underqualified to cook a delicious meal, so you buy more QVC gadgets and a new set of pots and pans to make up for your perceived inadequacies.

---

* I'm now realizing how aggressively that game is based on gender stereotypes.

You add to feel satisfied, but it's an empty, fleeting satisfaction.

And now you have more noise to manage.

True fulfillment comes from *subtraction,* from removing everything that distracts you from what matters and leaving only what's *essential.*

That's the root of essentialism, and I'm so grateful Greg McKeown was smart enough to turn the concept into a verb so you and I can have better lives, embracing what matters and ditching what doesn't. McKeown wrote, "An Essentialist makes trade-offs deliberately."[5]

So does a Lazy Genius. I know it's discouraging to remove items and appointments and even relationships that prevent you from living a life that matters to you. Adding is fun. Buying stuff is fun. I went into Hobby Lobby yesterday to buy watercolor paper for my kids and had to force myself to leave with only what I came for.

Am I a bad person for wanting to buy another white ceramic animal to put on my desk? Of course not. But by essentializing, I'm making trade-offs. I'd rather have surfaces that are less cluttered and therefore easier to clean than another knickknack. I'd rather add that twelve dollars to our family road trip fund than spend it on a quick purchasing high.

> True fulfillment comes from *subtraction,* from removing everything that distracts you from what matters and leaving only what's *essential.*

The purchasing itself isn't the problem. I still buy stuff and love it. But knowing and naming what matters helps me choose only what's essential.

Subtracting noise adds meaning to what you already have.

Stick with what's essential.

THE POWER TO CHOOSE

I can't begin to know the details of how and why you live the way you do, but it's also fair to assume you might have forgotten you have the ability to decide how you live. You have more control over your choices than you realize, as long as you *remember* to choose.

In Lazy Genius Principle #2, we talked about the power of starting small, how small decisions have a huge impact. It's easy to do and buy and schedule the way you always have, but if what you're choosing is unessential, you're choosing noise.

You can choose differently.

However, when I say you have a choice, I'm speaking to whether you buy or make cupcakes for a company Christmas party, whether you decide to redecorate your bedroom, and what you choose not to buy so you can save up to see the Pacific Northwest for the first time.

When I talk about supporting what matters, it's important to acknowledge that what matters is personal and greatly affected by our place in society and the world. And while I care deeply that we all live from a place of wholeheartedness, I recognize that my perspective on this is strongly influenced by the fact that I'm a middle-class white woman in America. I have a carport and a vacation fund and have never had to give up dinner so my own kids could eat. I have the luxury of crafting a meaningful life, of thinking about how many cardigans I want to own. I live with great privilege, and you might too.

You also might not.

Our individual abilities to choose are affected by issues like marginalization, abuse, trauma, and bias. I grew up in an abusive home, and choice wasn't always part of the equation. Not to be a downer, but it's an important thing to acknowledge.

Yes, we all live with choice, but some people have an easier path to implementing those choices than others. I simply want you to know that I see that reality and I see you.

Yet no matter the shape and speed of our lives, we all long for meaning. We want our time on this earth, in our homes, and with our people to matter.

So let's essentialize.

HOW TO KNOW IF SOMETHING IS ESSENTIAL

A few years ago, I wanted to learn how to knit. I went to the craft store and bought a dozen skeins of beautiful yarn and half a dozen needles in varying sizes, and I found a handful of blogs with patterns to try. Did I learn to knit? Um, no. Because I didn't essentialize.

I knew that learning to knit mattered. But why? In hindsight, I know it was to add simplicity to my life, to have something I could do quietly and mindlessly at the end of the day. But at the time, I didn't name it.

You have to know *why* something matters in order to know what's essential.

What I needed was one simple project to learn how to knit. What was essential to supporting that? One ball of yarn, one set of needles, and one highly rated YouTube tutorial.

What I got instead was chaos, not calm. I had too many choices and therefore too many distractions from what was essential. I didn't start small. And I never learned to knit.

I made the process too noisy to remember what mattered.

Here's another example: I used to have an entire cabinet shelf filled with different kinds of tea. Does tea matter to me? Actually, yeah. I love the liturgy of making a hot cup of tea on a cold afternoon. It slows me down, and that matters.

What doesn't matter is having fifteen different tea flavors to choose from. I always choose Earl Grey anyway, so why do I keep buying other teas? They're unessential, and all they do is create noise.

Making tea matters, and I'm more likely to make tea if I don't have to dig through a shoebox of tea bags to find my beloved Earl Grey.

A choice is essential only if it directly adds value to what matters *to you.*

ESSENTIALIZE IN THREE STEPS

McKeown lays out three steps for naming what's essential, and I'll do the same, adapted for living a Lazy Genius life. When you're choosing the essentials for a room, a habit, or a relationship, consider these:

1. Name what really matters.
2. Remove what's in the way.
3. Keep only the essentials.

Our guest bathroom is a bit of an eyesore, and if I forget what matters in that space, I will add noise and stress and plenty of nonessentials.

Allow me to give you a tour. There's a weird window that's not really a window even though it has actual shutters on it, and the paint is aggressively peeling off.

The wall next to the toilet is covered in pencil indentations because one of my boys did his math homework while taking care of business and didn't have scrap paper, so he used the wall.

The actual wall.

There's also a discarded nightstand that doesn't really go with the decor, but we stuck it there because we needed a place to store towels and toilet paper and didn't want to buy something new.

Clearly, the bathroom is not in its ideal state, but guess what?

It doesn't matter.

The first step is to name what matters. What matters about our guest bathroom is that it offers a clean, functional, reasonably pleasant experience for whomever uses it.

The second step is to remove what's in the way of that— the hand towel covered in toothpaste, the stack of *Calvin and Hobbes* books on the floor,* and my expectations of the bathroom looking like Joanna Gaines designed it.

The third step is to keep only the essentials: good-smelling soap, ample toilet paper, a bottle of Poo-Pourri in plain sight in case somebody has business to do, and a container of Clorox wipes in the nightstand cabinet to make cleaning quick and easy.

Sure, the bathroom might resemble a "before" photo on a home makeover show, but the essentials are covered, and that's what matters.

Every day, I save myself a lot of physical and mental energy by choosing to be okay with the bathroom as it is, by choosing what matters to me and ignoring the rest. Maybe the time will come when it matters more, but right now it doesn't.

Does that mean if you want an "after"-photo bathroom in your home, one of us is right and the other is wrong? Definitely not. It's easy to get sucked into what matters to someone else, but it has no bearing on what matters to you. Remember, choosing what matters to you doesn't make you better or worse than someone who chooses differently.

---

*The kids' bathroom reading, not mine.

Now let's look at some other examples of how essential-izing works in real life.

Essentializing Case Study #1: Getting Dressed

Since I don't know you or your closet, I'll use my own as an example.

First, I need to name what matters about getting dressed. That's easy—I want to easily choose clothes that make me feel like myself. It matters that the decision is effortless and that the first outfit I try is the one I end up wearing.

Second, I need to remove what gets in the way. For me, this includes excess choice, clothes that don't fit well, and clothes that aren't exactly my style.

Third, I need to keep only the essentials, which include all my favorite black, white, and denim clothing. I don't feel like myself when I wear color. Give me pre-Oz Kansas, please.

Now my closet and the process of getting dressed are es-sentialized. I've identified what matters to me and have made my environment match that by keeping only what's essential and getting rid of everything else.

Here's what's great. If having lots of clothing options mat-ters to you because you love to creatively express yourself through what you wear, your essential closet will look differ-ent from mine, and *it should*.

Don't assume essential means minimal, especially if you love a big closet filled with choices.

Essentializing Case Study #2: Spending Money

I won't put words in your mouth when it comes to your money, so we'll talk about mine instead.

First, Kaz and I need to name what matters with our money. We want to be faithful with what we have. I realize that's such a Sunday school answer, but it's the truth. As a couple, we've run the gamut of financial situations. We've both been in school at the same time, eating more cheap pasta than anyone should. We've lived on a first-year public school salary, where every single penny mattered. We have more freedom now because we're both contributing to our bank account, but in every situation, we want to be faithful with what we've been given. What matters to us is making responsible choices, giving generously, and using our money to experience the world as a family.

Second, we need to identify what we can remove that's in the way of what matters. The answer is anything that keeps us from being thoughtful with our spending: making impulsive purchases, buying something we don't need simply because it's on sale, or forgetting that every cent can make a big difference.

Third, we need to keep only the essentials. Based on what matters, the biggest essential is tracking what we spend. If I forget to input an expense into my budget app, I often put off entering the next one. And then the next one. A week later, I'm sitting with a purse full of receipts and limited understanding of where we are in our weekly spending. It's essential that I track our spending as we go so we stay in line with what matters.

You'll likely desire some level of thoughtfulness in your spending too, and it'll be much easier to stick to it if you know what matters. If you say "I want to spend more wisely" without any concrete reason, you won't essentialize.

Essentializing Case Study #3: Cleaning the Bathroom

I don't think I have adequate words to describe how much I hate cleaning the bathroom. It's dusty and wet and full of too many unmentionable substances, and I always feel like I need to take a shower when I'm done.

Still, we need clean bathrooms, at least most of the time. How can I essentialize the process so I'll do it more often without wanting to cut off my hands?

First, I need to name what matters about cleaning the bathroom. What matters is that I'm out of there as soon as humanly possible.

Second, I need to ask myself what I can remove that's keeping me from what matters. For one thing, I have too many choices of cleaners to use. Sometimes I even forget where the cleaners are, so I need to remove that obstacle by simplifying my cleaning products. I also can remove my repulsion by not waiting until the bathroom is disgusting.

Third, I need to keep only what's essential. Based on what matters and the obstacles keeping me from it, my essentials are cleaning the bathrooms once a week before they get too nasty, keeping them as tidy as possible in the meantime so I can clean more quickly, and having one cleaner in the bathroom so I'm not hunting around and losing my nerve to actually clean.

YOU CAN ESSENTIALIZE ANYTHING

Does your silverware drawer make you crazy? Maybe it's too full because you still feel compelled to take free stuff from anyone who offers and you now have way more cutlery than you need.

Does your makeup make you crazy? Maybe you use only five products but have to sort through thirty to find them.

Does the car pool line make you crazy? Maybe you're forgetting that picking up your kid every day and welcoming her into your minivan with a smile is more important than being annoyed with how poorly the line is set up in the first place.

Remember, in all things, start small. You don't have to essentialize every nook and cranny of your life today, but if you feel the distracting itch of real or emotional clutter, essentialize that space.

TO RECAP

- Essential doesn't have to mean minimal; it simply means eliminating distraction from what matters.
- Name what matters, remove what gets in the way, and keep only the essentials.
- You get to choose. Don't let someone else choose what matters to you.
- You can essentialize anything, so don't hesitate to try. Just start small.

— ONE SMALL STEP —

Essentialize your silverware drawer.

Once you have a home that's moving toward what's essential (remember, don't do it all at once), you'll find that certain tasks are much easier. Still, sometimes the order in which you do things matters, regardless of how much you've essentialized your life.

Next up, we'll discuss going in the right order.

GO IN THE RIGHT ORDER

Lazy Genius Principle #11

In the early years of marriage, I noticed that Kaz would hand-wash dishes before the dishwasher was full.

I'm sorry, *why*?

It felt like utter madness to me. Didn't he realize he might wash something he didn't have to? There's still room in that magical machine, New Husband. What are you doing?!

It drove me bonkers.

In hindsight, he *was* going in the wrong order, but so was I. While he started with the wrong task, I started with the wrong mind-set.

Going in the right order helps with efficiency, but if you make efficiency your primary goal, you're leaning too hard into genius territory. You're trying too hard at the wrong things and will only end up mad at your helpful husband because he's not efficient.

The lazy way is more than likely a default mind-set than an active choice. You might not be giving up on doing things in the right order; you simply weren't aware there was one. Some people's brains aren't wired to see tasks that way.

If that's you, I hope this chapter gives you a window into

how going in the right order can benefit your life in ways you didn't realize were possible.

If you're a genius when it comes to order, we'll start with this.

THE RIGHT ORDER FOR EVERYTHING

Any task, from filling out a spreadsheet to having a hard conversation, can be improved by following these three steps:

1. Remember what matters.
2. Calm the crazy.
3. Trust yourself.

A CRASH COURSE IN PERSPECTIVE

Assuming you might still need a little help naming what matters, especially concerning annoying things like chores, here are some ideas.

Tidying up isn't picking up your family's mess over and over again because they're ungrateful animals and you have to do everything. Tidying up is making space for a new, purposeful mess.

Changing the sheets isn't creating a visual upheaval of every single room. Changing the sheets is offering the comfort of climbing into a clean bed.

Exercise isn't something you have to do to get thin and be accepted. Exercise is the liturgy of tending to your body and releasing stress.

The lack of tangible steps is killing you, isn't it? I'm not going to tell you to just whistle while you work and everything will be fine, but your practical, daily tasks will have more impact if you begin here.

STEP #1: REMEMBER WHAT MATTERS

The Lazy Genius Way hinges on first remembering what matters. If you start anywhere else, you're starting from the wrong place. By remembering what matters in any task, you can easily see what's essential and what's not, what you can do now

Doing laundry isn't a referendum on how in control of your life you are. Doing laundry is a chance to refill closets with clothes that help you and your people feel comfortable and express yourselves.

Cleaning the kitchen isn't enduring an endless chore. Cleaning the kitchen is clearing space and stocking cabinets and drawers with food and tools to create connection around the table.

Pulling weeds in the yard isn't a punishment (except when I was a kid and I told a lie). Pulling weeds is an opportunity to make room for your favorite flowers to grow.

Cleaning your house isn't a constant burden on your shoulders. Cleaning your house is a way to tend to your home and make space for what matters.

to make things easier later, how your season of life is affecting the task, and any number of Lazy Genius principles.

Always start with what matters.

STEP #2: CALM THE CRAZY

Once you remember what matters and give yourself a good ol' reframe, you can move on to the next step: calm the crazy. Ultimately, this is the goal in life, right? You're tired of feeling like a headless chicken or a hamster on a wheel. You want far less crazy and way more calm.

When you're beginning a task, remember what matters and then ask yourself, *What one thing can I do that will most calm the crazy?*

We already talked about this with the Lazy Genius principle of building the right routines, and it even holds hands a little with the Magic Question. If you start a task with one thing that makes an immediate impact, you can calm the crazy more quickly and hopefully even enjoy what you're doing.

STEP #3: TRUST YOURSELF

Once you've remembered what matters and you've calmed the crazy, you will likely intuitively know what to do next. But you have to trust yourself.

You might find that easier said than done, especially if your voice isn't always trusted by others, like when you tell your doctor something isn't right in your body and he tells you to get more sleep. Or when you vulnerably tell a friend something you've discovered about your personality and she flippantly responds, "Oh, I don't see you that way."

If others don't trust your voice, it's really easy to dismiss it yourself.

However, you *can* trust yourself. In fact, it's vital that you do.

Over the years, I've created a handful of resources for women to help make their lives easier, and most of them require filling something out. Do you know how often women refuse to write anything down because they're afraid they'll do it wrong? Would you believe I receive multiple questions a day about how I personally do a task because so many women are insecure in their own choices?

You can trust yourself.

You know your life and your personality far better than I do, and therefore *you are the best person to know what you need.* Yes, others have beautiful insight, and it's a gift to listen and receive it, but not at the expense of your own voice.

You know your life and your personality far better than I do, and therefore *you are the best person to know what you need.* Yes, others have beautiful insight, and it's a gift to listen and receive it, but not at the expense of your own voice.

Trust yourself.

Even if we're talking about going in the right order with something as basic as laundry, your voice matters. Without trusting yourself, you'll hear my suggestion as a rule, even though your gut knows what you need better than I do.

We'll get into specific, practical ways to go in the right order, but every order begins best with these three steps:

1. Remember what matters.
2. Calm the crazy.
3. Trust yourself.

CASE STUDY #1: PUTTING AWAY MARKERS

My kids color all the time, so we have a lot of markers. I've spent hundreds of afternoons picking up dozens of them and their lonely tops from under chairs, behind curtains, and in my nightmares.

Seriously, why can't these tiny humans stop giving me stuff to do?

You guys use too many markers!

But my kids love art. They love to color and imagine and draw their own comics.

When I start with what matters, my perspective shifts and I'm far less angry. Rather than seeing the daily marker pickup as annoying, I see it as resetting what matters—creativity.

Next, I ask what I can do to calm the crazy of the markers, and the answer is to create an easy place for them to go. (And there's a nod to putting everything in its place. You see how all these principles play with one another?)

For a while, the markers were in their torn boxes, stuffed in different drawers, and hanging out in kids' rooms. It wasn't unusual to find multiple markers in my bathroom. I mean, *why*?

So we calmed the crazy. We got a giant basket for markers and cleared space for it next to the kitchen table where the kids usually color. Everyone now knows to dump every single marker in that basket.

Now it's time to trust myself on what comes next. Next steps aren't always formulaic, and that's true with our marker situation. However, now that I've remembered what matters and calmed the crazy, I can *see*. I notice that the biggest reason so many markers end up on the floor is because they're dried out. Of course a kid is going to chuck a useless marker on the floor! My next step is really obvious now that I can see: purge the dry markers. I don't need to google "marker storage" or look for creative solutions on Pinterest. All I need to do is remember what matters, calm the crazy, and trust myself to know what step to choose next.

Maybe this approach to your to-do list or to challenges you face feels overly emotional or simplistic, but in your usual method, you're likely overwhelmed by all the options and you don't know where to begin.

Go in the right order: Start with what matters. Calm the crazy. Trust yourself.

CASE STUDY #2: CLEANING THE HOUSE

Cleaning the entire house is a formidable mountain to climb, and it's hard to know where to start.

Start with what matters.

If cleaning your house is tending to your home and making space for what matters, think about that for a minute. Breathe. Give gratitude a second to take root. I know you're busy and don't have time to burn sage every time you need to vacuum, but remembering what matters is vital in knowing when to ditch a task and when to embrace it.

After you remember what matters about a clean house, think about what would calm the crazy. Your answer will be different from everyone else's because we all feel crazy over different things.

I have the clearest memory of an episode of *The Oprah Winfrey Show* where an audience member said she cleaned naked. When it was time to clean the house, she'd take off all her clothes and get to work. Why? She felt gross when she cleaned and didn't want that distraction. Apparently, cleaning without underwear on calmed this lady's crazy. It takes all kinds, my friend.

What room, if it was cleaned up, would make the house feel less crazy to you? What singular task would make that room feel less crazy? Calm the crazy.

For me, the answer is always the living room floor. When the toys and books and socks and measuring cups my daughter pulled out of the drawer are scattered about our main living space, I feel like my head is spinning without my permission. When it's tidy, I'm chill. That singular task of cleaning up the living room floor changes how I feel about the entire house.

Now it's time to trust what should come next. I don't need to seek out someone else's permission or even focus on what's *best*. Doing whatever feels right is a good next step based on what I need, how much time I have, and what energy I'm prepared to expend.

DON'T ALWAYS CLEAN THE DIRTIEST THING

You might think you need to clean whatever room has had the least amount of attention since the last time you cleaned. If you base your choice only on what's dirtiest, you might waste your time on a room that doesn't matter. Skip the dirtiest room if it keeps you from tending to a space that makes you and your house feel calmer.

The dirty room can wait.

CASE STUDY #3: CLEANING THE BATHROOM

You already know how much I hate this horrible room. Why is it the worst to clean?*

I won't lie; it's hard for me to remember what matters in the bathroom because the payoff isn't quick enough. Still, I know I will feel significantly better once it's clean and smells good. That promise pushes me through.

In terms of calming the crazy, the thing that drives me nuts is wet dust.

Think about when you clean the bathroom. You spray the sink or the toilet with cleaner and start wiping. But then there are these little pieces of blue and gray dirt that keep moving around! What's happening?

It's dust, and you just made it wet.

Rage core activated.

I feel crazy when my efforts to clean the bathroom seem pointless because I can't get rid of this wet dust, so the best way for me to calm the bathroom crazy is to dust first.

No sprays. No wet rags. Get everything off the surfaces and dust them.

Your way of calming the crazy will likely be different from mine, but that wet dust is an aggressive trigger for my anger. It makes sense for me to put this first, not only to make the cleaning process easier but also to make my attitude better.

Then I do whatever I think should naturally come next, which is usually quickly wiping down the surfaces.

The bathroom is acceptably clean, and I'm not angry. Mission accomplished.

---

*I can think of several reasons, and most involve the word *urine*.

A GOOD ORDER FOR GETTING THE BATHROOM EXTRA CLEAN

1. *Wipe off the dust.*

2. *Clear off all the surfaces.*

3. *Spray everything down and leave it.*

4. *Sweep or Swiffer the floor.*

5. *Wipe down the sink and toilet.*

6. *Clean the mirrors.*

7. *Scrub the tub and shower.*

8. *Mop the floor.*

9. *Put every bottle and brush back in its place.*

10. *Take a shower because you deserve it.*

CASE STUDY #4: LAUNDRY

Laundry definitely matters because we need to wear clothes. Beyond that, I love thinking about laundry as a way to replenish something that helps me and my people feel comfortable. When I go through the motions of sorting, washing, and putting away clothes with that perspective in mind, I can more easily find the joy in the task.

Once you remember what matters to *you* about laundry (because it could be something very different), ask yourself what you can do to calm the crazy.

LAUNDRY TIPS

Your needs are different based on what you're washing and how much time you have, but consider these tips to find your right order for laundry:

- **Start with sheets.** *They're a load on their own, and you can get a jump on washing clothes without waiting to gather everything else. Chances are you have all the sheets without needing to search the house for strays.*

- **Choose the next load to wash based on what you'll be doing when that load is finished drying.** *If the next dryer buzz will happen when you're leaving to pick up kids from school, don't wash a load of hanging clothes that will inevitably get wrinkled waiting for you to get home.*

- **Do your laundry overnight.** *If you gather and sort at night, wash a load that can get wrinkled and let it dry while you're sleeping. Load up the washer with the next load before you head to bed and then press the button to start it when you wake up. You're already a load and a half in before you've even had your coffee.*

It all depends on what makes you *feel* crazy.

For me, if I've put effort into sorting and washing based on where the clothes end up (remember batching?), I want that effort to pay off. It drives me bananas to begin a load of socks and underwear, only to find a dirty pair of socks somewhere else in the house.

I calm the crazy by gathering every single piece of dirty laundry from the house before I begin the first load. Otherwise, I lose the power of batch-sorting because I don't have all the clothes together at once.

After that, I trust myself to do whatever makes the most sense. Shocker: it's likely actually washing a load of laundry, but I can decide which load makes the most sense for how my day looks and how I'm feeling.

CASE STUDY #5: PLANNING YOUR DAY

Productivity doesn't always have to be the goal of your day.

It's okay to have a day that's full of resting or holding a baby or never even glancing at a to-do list. If you hold productivity as the standard for planning your day, you could be missing out on what actually makes it worthwhile.

Remember what matters, and you get to decide what that is.

Certain days need to be productive. If you're on a deadline, I understand the push to perform. Productivity itself isn't bad. But it's not what *always* matters.

As you plan your day either the night before or bleary eyed in the morning, first remember what matters that day: connection, cleaning the house so you'll feel more like yourself, getting a run in so you can work some stress out of your body, or stocking the freezer because you're about to hit a crazy time of life and need to Magic Question your meals for a bit.

What matters can be practical, soulful, or tangible. Or it could be a frustrated grab for anything resembling serenity. Whatever it is, *name it.*

Next, what can you do to calm the crazy for today? Fill in the blank on that one. You'll feel crazy for different reasons day to day, but by starting with what matters, you can answer that question more thoughtfully and do one thing to help you feel more like yourself as the day goes on.

Finally, trust yourself. Trust that you know what to embrace on your list and what needs to wait until another day. Trust that your people value you for reasons beyond what you do. Trust that you can get a grocery pickup on the way home from soccer practice and eat whatever you unpack since being together is what matters, not an Instagram-worthy dinner.

WHEN ORDER IS IN CHARGE

Maybe you feel inspired to go in this order: remember what matters, calm the crazy, and trust yourself. It feels whole-hearted and warm to me.

And yet . . .

I wish my husband would load the dishwasher before washing dishes.

I wish my son would realize that washing his hands *before* he uses the bathroom is actually a waste of time.

I wish I wouldn't get so riled up when my shopping list doesn't follow the same order as the grocery store aisles.

Depending on the system and on order itself leaves us hollow and robotic, even if we're technically getting a lot done.

I wish I didn't so often depend on order to lead me to a productive, successful day.

Life is nuanced and personal. I can't assume today's approach to my day will work tomorrow. I don't know if a kid will stay home sick from school, if I'll have a headache that knocks me out, or if unexpected road construction will send me into an irrational tizzy.

You and I can't depend on order as law. Depending on the system and on order itself leaves us hollow and robotic, even if we're technically getting a lot done.

I know you want the best way to do things. I'm guessing that even though this idea of the right order is appealing, it might also strike you as annoying.

Just tell me what to do, Kendra, and I'll do it!

You don't need me to tell you what to do, but I will offer you permission to trust yourself.

You know what to do better than I do because this is *your* life.

TO RECAP

- You know what you need more than any other person.
- Any task can go in the right order: remember what matters, calm the crazy, and trust yourself.
- Even though order is a beautiful thing, it's not the only thing.

— ONE SMALL STEP —

If you have a to-do list for today, pick one thing and go through these three steps. Pay attention to how your attitude and even your efficiency are affected by going in the right order.

On days when productivity isn't the ultimate goal, what is? Rest.

Let's talk about how to schedule it.

SCHEDULE REST

Lazy Genius Principle #12

About every month, I get what I call a body shutdown. It's like I have the flu—achy joints, chills, a headache, usually something gross and stomach related—but I don't actually have the flu.

What I have is a tired body that can't go on anymore.

Before I had kids, I did a better job of resting, even if it was accidental. I simply had more time. I would sleep in on the weekends, I could lean into my body's natural rhythms, and I didn't have a job with demanding hours. It was easier to rest, even if I didn't know the importance of it.

Then I had children, and all that time got sucked out the window.

This isn't a new story. If you have kids, you've experienced it. Or you might have a parent who needs around-the-clock care, a job with demanding hours, a business you started that you love but have to care for like it's a human.

Most of us have some kind of roadblock to rest.

The irony is that people with roadblocks generally need rest even more.

WHY WE NEED REST

This is obvious, right? Yet it's a principle so easily ignored.

If you want to embrace what matters, you need mindfulness to do it. If you want to get stuff done, you need energy to do it. Both of these are fueled by rest.

> **If you want to embrace what matters, you need mindfulness to do it. If you want to get stuff done, you need energy to do it. Both of these are fueled by rest.**

You already know that sleep heals wounds, reduces inflammation, gives your heart a break, and regulates hormones. We need sleep to function well. I'm guessing you won't argue with that.

But here's where the problem lies: you don't think sleep and rest are worthwhile.

You'll tell me there's too much to do, too many people to care for, and too many shows to watch, even though your eyelids are heavy. You might also think that because you've survived this long on your current rhythm of rest, you might as well keep going. Sure, you're tired and cranky, but it's mostly manageable, right?

I thought that too, until my body turned on me.

THE IDEAL VIEW OF REST

For a while, my body shutdowns became more frequent, once every couple of weeks. Then I had a couple of panic attacks where I couldn't breathe and had to call someone to come get me.

I would deal with the situation only when it presented itself. For a body shutdown, I'd call Kaz to come home early to be with the kids, rub grapefruit essential oil on my stomach, take three ibuprofen, and then crash for twelve hours. For the panic attacks, I'd breathe through them, mostly recover, and occasionally make an appointment with my counselor if it felt appropriate.

Instead of paying attention to the root problem, I was dealing only with the immediate symptoms. If I did think about a long-term solution, it was always too big:

Gosh, I need a vacation.

I need to get away.

I need a long stretch of time when I can relax and have zero responsibilities.

Then I'd vow to buy a book on morning rituals and google "tips to get more sleep." I thought the solution to my body shutdowns was to be a genius about rest, gathering as many hacks and tips as I could while I waited for my big vacation to arrive.

What about you? When you think about rest, what do you see?

Maybe it's an empty room that doesn't belong to you, a plush white bed, curtains blowing in the breeze. Maybe you see the ocean or the mountains. You see a weekend alone in a cabin in the woods or a girls' trip eating and shopping and sleeping in. So many beautiful possibilities, and none include overbearing bosses or tiny children.

It's pretty common to imagine rest on a grand scale. If you could get away for a while, everything would be better. All you need is a break.

The irony is that when you do get the opportunity—when the grandparents take the kids for a sleepover or you get invited on a girls' weekend—you get stressed out trying to rest.

Make it count! This is the only chance you'll get for seven more years!

Then you return home, and life is mostly the same, even though you just got away from it all.

Why?

You don't know how to rest.

Amid the daily grind, you've grown lazy about rest. You live and survive and do your best, waiting desperately for a break that feels like it will never come. And that all-or-nothing mentality always leaves you discontent. If you want a day to yourself, getting only an hour is a letdown. If you dream of a weeklong vacation on a tropical island, an overnight hotel stay in your own town is disappointing. No form of rest seems enough, and this discontent can even morph into *life* not being enough, which means we must be doing something wrong, which means *we* are not enough.

It's so fun to be a person, isn't it?

THE TRUTH ABOUT SELF-CARE

In order to be a Lazy Genius about rest, you have to name what matters to you, do it, and let the other concerns fall away. I find this simple perspective to be helpful when discussing self-care.

Self-care is as trendy as cold-shoulder shirts and Paleo.* The latest hype is to take time for yourself and meet your own needs so you can be a better, healthier person. Examples include using weekly facial masks, getting a manicure, or going for a run. They often focus on the physical body and even skew a little toward pampering. While I am all about the pampered life, it's not always practical on a daily basis, nor does it tackle the deeper reason you're tired.

---

* I'm writing this in 2019. Insert appropriate trends as you see fit.

Self-care should be a regular practice of doing what makes you feel like yourself. It's a practice of remembering who you are.

NAMING WHAT MAKES YOU FEEL LIKE YOURSELF

In the introduction, I said you're tired not because of your schedule but because you're trying so hard to be a perfectly optimized human. Sure, busy schedules play a role. On the other hand, for years I was busy only with dirty diapers and crying babies, yet I still felt as exhausted as if I'd been trading stocks or running an ER.

Your tasks aren't necessarily the origin of your stress; trying to fit into a mold of who you think you *should* be almost always is. You spend all day doing and managing and overthinking, and before long, you forget who you are in the midst of the madness.

You need a practice of remembering who you are and resting in your identity. There's more than one way to do this, so don't feel pressured to find the single, perfect thing that defines you. Your list will be long, and that's good.

When do you feel most alive?

What makes you confident and sure in who you are?

What can you do for hours without effort and feel all kinds of joy?

If you can name several practices that help you feel like yourself, that allow you to remember and rest in the truth of who you are, you'll experience a level of rest that can literally change your life.

Here's my personal list of what makes me feel like myself: baking, listening to music, walking or running in a natural setting, being with friends, laughing, feeding people, and noticing my surroundings.

What doesn't? Working in the yard, crafting, shopping, cleaning, and anything having to do with my nails.

Once you have your own list and know what does and doesn't make you feel like yourself, you're better equipped to develop rhythms of seasonal rest, weekly rest, daily rest, and soul rest.

Our lives aren't one size fits all, so our approaches to rest shouldn't be either.

Let's explore this more.

SEASONAL REST

Starting with a weekly day off or a daily act of rest might be too much too soon, so let's start with seasonal rest. I love the built-in rhythm of the seasons, and they can teach us a lot about cycles of life and taking a break.

So, right now, pull out your calendar and schedule a seasonal day of rest. If you're brave, go ahead and schedule enough for the entire year.

Set aside one day every three months to be your true self. Remember who you are, have fun doing what you like, and receive how much you're loved. Schedule the day so you'll honor it. Don't be lazy about it.

Your day of seasonal rest can be whatever you need it to be. That's the fun of being a Lazy Genius with self-care and rest. Do only what matters to *you*.

You can spend time reflecting, running, reading, or anything else you can think of that starts with *r*. (I mean, if we're not writing with alliteration, why are we even here?)

Take the time and do what makes you feel like yourself.

Lazy Geniuses start small, and creating a rhythm of four days of rest a year shouldn't be too big an ask.

WHEN YOU STRUGGLE TO TAKE TIME FOR YOURSELF

If you can't take even four days a year to claim time for yourself, there's something deeper at work.

Do you not feel like you're worth it?

Do you assume too much depends on you?

Do you value other people's needs over your own?

Intellectually, you know taking four days is not a lot to ask, but you might be too overwhelmed to actively pursue it.

This is your permission. You're allowed to require time for yourself. You're allowed to prioritize your own body and soul four days a year.

WEEKLY REST

The next step is weekly rest.

Does it have to be one entire day a week? Nah. That would be awesome, but it's better to do what's more likely to work than what's ideal.

Look at your list of what makes you feel like yourself, and consider one or two things that could fit into a weekly rhythm.

It might help to think about how the weekly rhythm would best work for you. Is it the day itself? Maybe you could use a midweek break on Wednesdays or an intentional day of rest on Sundays. Is it the activity regardless of what day it falls on? Maybe you would love going to Zumba once a week and there are options for choosing different class sessions depending on your schedule. Naming that difference can help.

My personal weekly rest is rooted more in my choices than in a day itself. I walk or run as a stress reliever three times a week, but those three times don't have to be on specific days or even be spaced out that well. Last week, I ran on Thursday, Friday, and Saturday, which is spaced out as little as logistically possible. Still, it counts, and it helps. I feel more like myself when my stress has somewhere to go, and it's a bonus when I get to run in the woods.

Your weekly rest could be as simple as getting coffee at a local shop and taking it to the farmers' market every Saturday morning. You could go for a long walk one morning when your kids are in preschool, or you could pull weeds after dinner one or two nights a week.

Small steps matter, and fitting them into your week doesn't have to be complicated. Start with one activity and do it weekly.

DAILY REST

One of my favorite things in all the world is to bake. Give me an afternoon to make bread or a pie and feed it to my people? Yes, please. It makes my body relax and my soul feel at peace more than most things do.

But can I do that every day? Definitely not. Baking takes

time, and while I do make time for what matters, I can't from a practical standpoint give baking daily attention.

I think that's where we get stuck on daily rest. Your daily thing doesn't have to be your favorite thing. If you hold your absolute favorite way to rest as the goal, especially when it's tough to find time for it on a daily basis, you'll be disappointed and think daily rest isn't in the cards for you.

But it *needs to be.*

Start small.

Maybe instead of baking a pie every day, I can flip through a baking cookbook and dream about what I'll make next. If you love to run on the beach but live several hours from the coast, run while listening to ocean sounds. (Don't knock it till you try it.)

> **Your daily thing doesn't have to be your favorite thing.**

Small, intentional, daily acts of rest are way more powerful than those magical unicorn weekends without kids or responsibilities, because you're learning *how* to rest.

Find small, simple ways to engage in something that makes you feel like yourself, even if it's not your ideal activity. There's something you can do every day, so schedule it and do it as often as you can.

DAILY REST VIA SLEEP

I'm not going to tell you to go to bed earlier or charge your phone in a separate room. If those work for you, awesome, but that's not the point here.

Let's use another Lazy Genius principle and go in the right order. Always start with what really matters. Maybe you need a reframe on what matters about sleep. Instead of seeing it as something you just do or as a waste of time, think of sleep as a way to refuel yourself.

You matter, and your sleep matters too.

Are there trade-offs? Sure.

THERE'S ALWAYS ONE SET OF FOOTPRINTS

My personal efforts to gain control are connected to my spiritual life with Christ, and in case that's true of you too, I'd love to share my feelings about the poem "Footprints in the Sand." You know the one I mean, right? I think it hit peak bookmark exposure around 1995.

The author of the poem describes a dream in which her life is a walk on the beach with God. When she was happy and serene, there were two sets of footprints, side by side. But during the hardest, saddest times of her life, only one set was visible. When she asks God why he left her when life was most difficult, he replies that he never left; he was carrying her. The footprints were his.

The last lines are like an M. Night Shyamalan twist for Christians.

I admit that as a young, spiritually frothy teenager, this poem blew my mind. What a mic drop. He carries me during the hard times? What a kind, loving God I serve!

I'm a huge sports fan, and some of my favorite NBA match-ups don't tip off until ten thirty. Um, that's *late*. Is it worth sacrificing feeling like myself? Sometimes yes; usually no. By naming what really matters (rest trumps basketball), I can choose what makes sense for me.

> *But wouldn't it be great if our walk was mostly two sets of footprints? Doesn't that feel right? He'd obviously like me more if I didn't need him so much.*
>
> *For most of my life, that was my goal. Needing God was acceptable for the really hard things, but I did everything I could to make it work on my own.*
>
> *And I was shockingly good at it.**
>
> *But I missed the part in Sunday school about how trying doesn't make me holier. It doesn't make Jesus prouder. It doesn't make me a better Christian.*
>
> *It just makes me tired.*
>
> *You depend on yourself until you can't anymore and then cry out for Jesus or a beach vacation. Exhaustion in both your body and soul catches up to you, and you're done.*
>
> *The truth is we will never reach the end of our need for him. And he will never tire of that need.*
>
> *There's always one set of footprints.*

*I was voted Most Dependable by my senior class. Most *Dependable*. That's about as perfect and unsexy as it gets.

And remember that the choice you make today doesn't have to be the choice you make tomorrow.

A helpful lens for seeing the value of sleep is remembering that I can bring today to an end, knowing that most likely I'll get another day tomorrow and can do with tomorrow whatever I like.

Maybe that's simplistic, but it makes a difference. I feel less pressure to fit everything into tonight, because tomorrow is coming. Sleep isn't something I finally succumb to because my body is telling me, *Kendra, get it together and close your eyes!* The process is slow and purposeful, and it actually pays off more when I see it as a switch I'm choosing to flip.

Today is done. Tomorrow will come. Time to go to sleep.

SOUL REST

Emily P. Freeman calls rest for your soul "sitting down on the inside."[6] I love that because I know exactly what it feels like to be standing, running around, or hiding in a corner on the inside.

Your inner life greatly influences your physical well-being, and when you don't give your soul a chance to rest, your body will feel it acutely. You have to stop carrying burdens you were never meant to carry. As long as you're weighed down on the inside, physical rest will go only so far.

For me, my soul finds rest in believing in my true identity. When I believe that I was made on purpose, that my personality is a gift, that I am enough as I am and not because of what I do, I'm able to more fully sit down on the inside. I can seek out connection rather than protection.

I can be myself and let go of what doesn't matter, which is almost always my trying to do everything on my own. When I try to handle it all, I can't receive help and let people in. I don't have enough mindfulness to pay attention to what the season is trying to teach me. I forget to start small. I go in the absolute wrong order, putting my productivity in the driver's seat.

Soul rest and learning to sit down on the inside are acts of letting go. You don't have to hold everything together. You can rely on people and a power bigger than you are.

If you're ignoring your own rest for the sake of something that doesn't matter, it's time to let go.

One of God's commands for his people, alongside don't kill people or cheat on your wife, is to remember the Sabbath day and keep it holy.

Rest is part of how we're made.

Set it apart.

Schedule it.

Honor it.

Don't carry and haul and try, only to end up emotionally exhausted by evening. Rest daily, weekly, seasonally, and in your soul, and experience the fullness of who you are.

TO RECAP

- Self-care is less about pampering than it is about doing what makes you feel like yourself.
- Rest doesn't happen on its own; you have to schedule it.
- Name what makes you feel whole, and find ways to experience what you named on a seasonal, weekly, and daily basis.
- Stop carrying what you were never meant to carry and instead sit down on the inside.

— ONE SMALL STEP —

Schedule a day for yourself in the next three months. Just one day.

You don't always have to do everything, but you probably still try. And you likely fail at it, same as me. If you have more practice at telling yourself what you did wrong than you do at being kind to yourself, this final principle is the best way to end.

BE KIND TO YOURSELF

Lazy Genius Principle #13

The other night, I was in a *place*. My emotions were throwing a tantrum, my hormones were into the drama, and my headstrong three-year-old daughter was the ringmaster of my personal torture. After a solid hour of hostage negotiations involving a decent bit of regrettable yelling (read: putting her to bed), I sank into my IKEA chair covered in Sharpie and pudding and said to my husband through tears, "I feel like such a terrible mom."

And he didn't respond.

Maybe he didn't hear me? [sniff, sniff]

Crickets.

And then I saw red. How dare he see through my emotional manipulation and not tell me exactly what I wanted to hear? How dare he let such a vulnerable statement hang in the air without swooping in to make me feel better? And I told him so. Angrily.

Several minutes later, after I had stopped yelling and remembered I was a grown-up who could apologize and use my words, I asked him why he didn't respond.

"Because I knew if I said you were a good mom, you'd throw it back at me."

Oh. Cool.

And he was totally right.

If Kaz had said, "Babe, you're such a great mom," I probably would've responded with some eye roll or wave of the hand, anything to shrug off what I actually wanted but didn't know how to receive.

I held myself to high mom standards and indirectly held my husband to high mind-reading standards and then put myself in a position to not be able to receive any kindness.

Why? Because in that moment, I felt like a really bad mom. That was my truth.

Did I want Kaz to help change that truth? Sure I did, but he was right that it wouldn't have mattered. I immediately dismiss so many affirmations of who I am because I'm not prepared to believe them.

> Without affection for ourselves, without softness on the inside, without being kind to ourselves, we will always be tired.

Without affection for ourselves, without softness on the inside, without being kind to ourselves, we will always be tired. We will always carry what we were never intended to carry and dig holes that go nowhere. Our energy goes to keeping up with our moving finish line, leaving no space for contentment and acceptance of who and where we are right now.

Oh, and bonus: when we're not loving ourselves, it's really hard to accept love from others.

THE LAZY GENIUS GOLDEN RULE

Naming what you want to embrace and what you want to ditch when it comes to chores and calendars feels a lot easier than naming what matters about *yourself.* The Golden Rule says to treat others the way you want to be treated, but I don't think you treat yourself super well. It's a hard rule to follow when the foundational half isn't always true.

Let's talk about how you treat yourself. How would you describe your relationship with yourself? Are y'all enemies? Rivals? Are you your own Jillian Michaels?

I'm guessing that you hold yourself to fairly high standards, that you're on a search for the optimized, ideal you. As long as you're *not* that ideal, either you'll try to be a genius about that future self, pushing and tracking and setting goals you don't reach, or you'll be lazy, seeing all growth as useless and finally quitting altogether.

Remember, we often think it's either try hard or give up.

Let's do it a different way.

You've likely heard on some girl-talk podcast that you should treat yourself the way you would a friend, but that's not the full picture. The Lazy Genius Golden Rule says that *you are your own friend.*

You're not a project.

You're not something to be fixed and sculpted and assessed on a daily basis.

You're a person of value as you are *right now,* and that person deserves your kindness because she is your friend.

CHILL OUT ON THE POTENTIAL

Would you look at a dear friend from the perspective of her potential—what she *could* be—and judge her for what she's not? Of course you wouldn't. That would be cruel.

But you do it to yourself. You regularly look from the perspective of your potential and assess what you could be or should be rather than look upon yourself with kindness and love.

I'm telling you, potential will eat your lunch.

You keep the future, ideal version of yourself as the carrot, and it leaves you discontent with who you are now. You don't look right, act right, dress right, or cook the right foods. You don't parent right, date right, read the Bible right, or know how to make great cupcakes from scratch. So you keep trying to become that person in the distance who knows how to do everything the right way, and you quietly chide yourself for who you are now and for not getting there quickly enough.

This is why habits and goals can feel so loaded. Daily habits usually serve to help us improve who we currently are or reach some kind of potential we're aiming for. Hear me. I'm not saying you shouldn't strive to grow, but if you seek some arbitrary ideal without being kind to who you are right now—to the person who is enough, who isn't just a shadow of who you're trying to be—that ideal will become an idol that keeps letting you down.

I believe deep in my bones that living by these Lazy Genius principles, even the super practical ones, will exercise the muscle of seeing yourself with kinder eyes as you rest, reflect, and walk a path toward a deeper, truer version of who you already are and what matters to you.

Let's all stop right here for a moment and learn to value who we are now, reflect on who we are becoming, and celebrate along the way. Here's how.

STEP #1: VALUE WHO YOU ARE NOW

A small way to value who you are now is with a daily act of kindness. Do something for yourself that's a gift to who you are *today*.

Don't be fooled and turn this into a genius thing. This act of kindness is not daily push-ups you've never cared about, daily journaling you've never found fulfillment in, or daily housecleaning because you should be on top of that more. It's not a daily habit of growth.

It's a daily act of kindness.

Think about what you do for a friend you love. You show up with coffee just because. You text her randomly to tell her you love her. You offer to take her kids with you on an errand so she can have an hour alone. None of those acts are meant to make her a better human or inspire her toward her potential. They show kindness simply because she's loved.

You can love yourself and show yourself genuine kindness too.

I know this is weird territory. I'm not saying you should look in the mirror and say "I love you" to the reflection, but it sure seems like a better idea than looking in the mirror and saying "Get it together," which I have 100 percent done.

Showing yourself kindness every day isn't meant to puff you up. It's meant to help you remember that you are made from and surrounded by the Divine and that he delights in you as you are.

Be kind to yourself, as you would be to a friend. Embrace the daily act of speaking to who you are today with compassion and excitement. Sit in silence, breathe in the early morning air, read a novel without justification, take a nap, accept a friend's offer to bring you dinner. Look in the mirror and smile at who you see. Not *what* you see, but *who* you see. You're not a blueprint seeking completion; you're a sacred soul created by the God of the universe.

Love who you are now. You're deserving.

STEP #2: REFLECT ON
WHO YOU ARE BECOMING

James Clear says, "If you want better results, then forget about setting goals. Focus on your system instead."[7]

That's a fun mic drop. Forget about setting goals? Yes, please!

And guess what? The book in your hands right now is teaching you *how to build a system,* how to create a structure and rhythm around what matters. If you start there rather than with the "after" photo, you'll be on a path to discovery of who you already are. You'll kindly love where you are and not be so weirded out by growing and becoming better.

As you create systems around what matters, don't focus so much on the endgame. Instead, think about how you can continue to grow comfortable in your own skin and enter a room with confidence and calm.

Embrace change. You can't be who you were at twenty when you're forty. For example, I can't try to be thinner than I've ever been, especially when the thinnest I've been was at age nineteen when I had an eating disorder and ate only eight hundred calories a day for over a year. It's ridiculous that I sometimes get annoyed with myself for not being that small anymore.

That was three babies and twenty years ago.

That's me looking back at a past "ideal," not kindly looking ahead and reflecting on who I am becoming.

Pay attention to your steps, to where you were a year ago and where you are today. It's not comparison for the sake of a sticker chart or some kind of hollow validation.

I, for instance, can celebrate that with this third baby, although I was still tired and kind of annoyed with diapers and sleepless nights, I was more settled in my own skin as a mother. That skin might look way different than I wish it did, especially during swimsuit season, but who cares?

Sure, I'm all about affirming a mother's body and the work it accomplished to grow an actual human person, but it's not even that. We need to stop putting ourselves on a spectrum of how we look and instead focus on how we feel. That statement might make you want to throw this book at my head, but when I think about how obsessed I've been, how much energy I've spent bashing myself for not looking like a CrossFit athlete when I don't do anything remotely close to CrossFit, I have to again practice being kind to myself.

I have weird defaults that make me compare myself to others. I've held myself to impossible standards and gotten angry at myself for not meeting them. I've slammed myself for not getting it together. I've marked those moments with angsty journal entries and insane exercise plans.

Ironically, I've given less attention to marking moments of personal growth, of newfound patterns of calm when I talk to my kids, of growth in my skills as a baker, of greater confidence in my voice in the room than I had ten years ago.

Compassionately reflecting on who you are becoming is such an act of kindness, and I'm still learning to practice this.

Mark the moments of growth and call them good.

We're kind to our friends. We cheer them on and champion their dreams. We sit with them in difficult situations and don't constantly offer ways to improve their lives. We hug them and bring them cups of coffee and look them in the eye and say "I love you." I would bet a lot of dollars that you don't speak or act this kindly to yourself much at all, if ever. And you definitely don't mark your own moments the way you do those of other people.

Be kind to yourself—with your words, in your pursuit of who you're becoming, and with grace when you take it slow.

SIMPLE WAYS TO BE KIND TO YOURSELF

- *Keep a journal and write about how you're doing, maybe even on your seasonal rest days.*

- *Take a walk and whisper a prayer of thankfulness for who you are.*

- *Look in the mirror and smile at yourself without judgment.*

- *Allow yourself space to sit without anything to show for it.*

- *Stop wearing clothes that don't fit or that don't make you feel like yourself.*

- *Stop critiquing every choice and how it affects the ideal, future you.*

STEP #3: CELEBRATE

My friend Francie, a wife and mom of two elementary-aged girls, went to nursing school as an adult, and it was hard. I casually say this from my own vantage point, not having lived through doing homework late at night, juggling who would pick up the kids on what days, finding babysitters when neither parent could get home in time, and generally struggling through the process even though it was the right path.

When Francie graduated from nursing school, she celebrated by inviting around forty friends to a big picnic shelter at the local park, where we ate barbecue and cake and gave a giant high five to our friend. Thinking about the sacredness of that day makes me teary.

To be a part of celebrating this huge undertaking my friend had accomplished? What a gift.

It would've been easy for Francie and her family to let the graduation slip by, to toast around the dinner table, or to order pizza from a fancy place instead of from the restaurant they had coupons for. Instead, they knew the road was hard and lovely and absolutely worth celebrating *with the people who love them*. It was so simple and so profound.

Letting people in and celebrating with them, both their triumphs and yours, is an exceptionally fun, special way to be kind to yourself. You don't have to be falsely extroverted to make this happen either. Big, small, seemingly insignificant . . . the size of the celebration and even what you're celebrating are irrelevant.

Just celebrate.

HOW TO CELEBRATE SOMETHING TODAY

I love throwing parties. Like, a lot.

I've thrown *Hunger Games* trivia parties, a *Wizard of Oz* costume party, and a carrot cake tasting party. I'm currently preparing for a board game Olympics party.

No one knows this, but I've thrown every party simply because I felt like celebrating *life*. It's my own personal form of celebration, of being kind to myself, of letting people in and feeding them cake until they burp.

Perhaps you think celebrating feels insignificant to Lazy Geniuses, but you, my friend, would be wrong. We embrace what matters, and gatherings, laughter, and growth matter.

Celebrating moments, with yourself and with others, makes you notice what matters. You give yourself permission to put flags in the sand. You create memories that encourage you through hard days and offer chances to laugh later in remembrance.

You get to publicly proclaim that what matters to you is important and valuable and worth celebrating. It's a tremendous act of kindness toward yourself.

So, right now, I want you to celebrate something.

Like, *today*.

I'm not saying you have to throw a massive party in three hours, but you can absolutely be kind to yourself right now by celebrating something on purpose.

Practically speaking, you'll need to decide three things: what to celebrate, how to celebrate, and who to celebrate with.

What to Celebrate

It could be that you've been working on something diligently for weeks, even though there aren't any results yet to show for it. It could be that you're living the life of a stay-at-home mom and feel more content than you did a few months ago. Or maybe you got an article accepted by a website, but it feels too small to really acknowledge.

Celebrate whatever feels important—tangible or intangible, on any point of the journey. Pick something that matters and celebrate it.

GET YOURSELF A PREZZIE

If you grew up with any kind of financial strain on the family or with parents who were frugal, the idea of actually buying something for yourself might feel ludicrous. In fact, this is the voice I hear in my head sometimes: What, I'm supposed to buy myself something every time I don't yell at my kid? You want me to go into credit card debt to celebrate stupid things?

No, Kendra, of course not, and I'm sorry I made you so angry.

A gift to yourself can be a kindness.

A present can act as a marker, as a reminder of that skill you thought you'd never learn. When you put on the shoes or wear the earrings or treat yourself to a fancy facial, you remember how good it felt to meet the sales goal at work, to finish the book proposal, to organize the enormous church clothing drive.

It's okay to get yourself a gift, especially when you can use that gift to remember who you are and what makes you come alive. You're a grown-up and can decide what's healthy and what's excessive, but there's a chance you aren't super generous toward yourself when it comes to giving prezzies.*

Get yourself a prezzie sometimes. It's a way to be kind.

---

*Jamie Golden, cohost of *The Popcast with Knox & Jamie,* calls presents "prezzies," and I can't not call them that now.

How to Celebrate

The cop-out, especially for celebration newbies, is to do a little cheer in your head and move on. While that has its own value, for today, get the celebration out of your head and into your world.

Celebrate with an impromptu dinner out with friends, a phone call, or a kitchen gadget you've had your eye on but never think is worth getting for yourself. Celebrate by inviting a friend over to watch a couple of episodes of *Poldark* while you eat fancy ice cream.

Celebrate by saying out loud to another human that you're proud of something you did. You're allowed to care about what matters, so show yourself kindness by validating that moment and its importance in your life.

Who to Celebrate With

And now the final ingredient of celebrations: the who. *Not the band, autocorrect* (although that would be a particular kind of celebration, to invite The Who).

Unless you're a hermit, this is the best part of the celebration. Push through the awkwardness of being vulnerable and invite your people to celebrate whatever you want to celebrate. It's worth it.

The best thing about celebrating with people is that you can't hide. You *have* to celebrate, and then you get to experience how fun it actually is.

My only advice is to celebrate with safe people. If you wonder if someone will quietly judge you for celebrating something that's not a birthday, maybe she's not the best person to include. You're already on baby deer legs when it comes to celebrating, so surround yourself with safe people who would celebrate anything with you because they love *you*.

CELEBRATING ISN'T A BURDEN

I'm writing this particular section of the book on the day I'm turning in my final manuscript. It's been a process, often a difficult one, and I've worked harder on this than I've ever worked on anything.

I've been cheered on by so many amazing people with GIFs, texts, flowers, coffee, and just being seen. Michael and Hannah are two of those friends. They have asked to celebrate every single step of this book with me and my family, even the ones I would've moved past without a second thought. We've shared meals and cake and in-the-flesh high fives. They've taught me the beauty of marking all these moments with a celebration.

So tonight we're going out for Greek food and maybe ice cream afterward. It's a small but mighty celebration of this thing I've done, this finish line I've crossed.

If I'm honest, I've often felt like a burden to them. Do they really care enough to give this kind of attention to something I would've moved right past? Apparently yes, and it's changed me.

Yesterday, Hannah said, "We will never get tired of celebrating you."

That's the kind of friend and celebrator I want to be.

Sure, it's easy to quickly cheer for yourself in your own head for three seconds, but maybe you would benefit from more celebration practice, like I have, in order to see how much you love and even need celebration in your life.

Marking significant moments is good for my soul. Celebrating my work and what matters to me is a way I've been able to show myself kindness, a practice I'm still learning. Plus, it's *fun*. I mean, I'm all for therapy and will champion it until I'm blue in the face, but despite its life-changing qualities, it's definitely not as fun as a party.

Don't miss out on this fun and simple way to be kind to yourself, and don't miss out on offering this kind of fun to your people.

Celebration is never a burden because *you are not a burden*. Be kind, be kind, be kind.

TO RECAP

- You are your own friend. You're worthy of kindness, especially from yourself.
- Value who you are now and lovingly accept yourself without comparison to the past or the future.
- Reflect on how you're becoming more of yourself.
- Celebrate one accomplishment that matters to you, today.

— ONE SMALL STEP —

Text a friend about a small victory. You could say something like, "Okay, this might be weird, but I went to Target with all three kids and didn't yell once or stress-buy anything. I'm feeling really proud of myself. Just wanted to share. Thanks for being the kind of friend who celebrates the little things with me."

Now that we've talked through all thirteen principles, it's time to put them all together and live like a Lazy Genius.

HOW TO LIVE
LIKE A LAZY GENIUS

Earlier, I said you don't need a new list of things to do but a new way to *see*. Now that you have these thirteen principles in your virtual Swiss Army knife, you can see every situation you face through a lens of embracing what matters and ditching what doesn't.

Let's walk through how to do this.

ALWAYS START WITH WHAT MATTERS

You can't do anything until you know what matters to you, but how do you actually know?

You have two choices: global reflection or mindfulness.

Global Reflection

Sit down with a notebook, make two columns—Lazy and Genius—and start writing down areas of your life in the appropriate columns.

The Genius column lists anything that makes you happy, that you want to cultivate and make more time for, that makes you feel like yourself, or that carries great importance to your family.

The Lazy column lists anything that saps you dry, that you constantly put off, or that you want to run away from.

What lights you up and what weighs you down?

Write it down. Name it.

The Genius column gives you a window into what matters so you can create space for it to grow.

But it's not the only way.

Mindfulness

If sitting down to list everything in your soul, your calendar, and your home is overwhelming, start small by being mindful.

Notice a time of day, a task, or an upcoming project that you'd like to Lazy Genius. You don't have to name what matters about everything . . . just *that* thing.

You can also be mindful of when you're frustrated, withdrawn, or angry. Did something trigger your negative response? Is there something earlier in the process that you can apply Lazy Genius principles to?

You can name what matters one situation at a time.

WHEN THE THINGS THAT MATTER TALK TO ONE ANOTHER

My personal Genius list includes a tidy space, feeding people, connection with my people, my home feeling comfortable to anyone who enters it, music, laughter, managing my stress well, celebrating and supporting my friends, plants I can keep alive, and James McAvoy (but there's only so much I can do about that one).

I could look for specific ways to be a genius about each

particular thing on my list, or I could notice which items are already talking to one another.

My list has a lot about my home and the feeling within its walls. Music, food, comfort, connection . . . apparently, I like a mood. But it's not just a feeling for feeling's sake. For me, it all comes down to the people.

If I notice how my list is one broader conversation, I can distill so much of what matters to me about my home into one value: it feels like home to everyone who walks inside.

I put a lot of effort into making that happen and use my quick fixes for things that matter less. Here are some ways I'm a genius about what matters:

- I spend time exploring recipes that comfort the body and the soul and learn to cook them well.
- I put energy into keeping my spaces tidy.
- I splurged on a good speaker system so that mood music fills the whole house with one click.
- I'm thoughtful about what I bring into my home so I can concentrate on making a room cozy rather than trying to cram more stuff into baskets and bins.
- I spend money on plants and candles because they make a room feel more welcoming.
- I invite people over as often as I can, opening our door no matter the state of our home and never apologizing for it.

I see other things on my list, like laughter and deep connection with friends and family, and notice another integration: I want people to feel at home not only in my *home* but also in our relationship, in their own skin, and in the safety of sharing their lives with me. That can happen in a conversation with a trusted friend, in an Instagram message with a stranger, or right here in the pages of this book.

By paying attention to what matters to me and how those values talk to one another, I've been able to name a life philosophy that affects every decision I make: *I want people to feel safe and at home with me.*

Obviously, others desire that too, but it's what I desire *most*.

Now I have a filter for what to embrace, what to ditch, and how I can better get stuff done.

Rather than life-hacking my way to being a person who does everything, I can be a genius about the things that matter most and give leftover attention to anything else.

Naming and embracing what matters changes everything.

LAZY GENIUS CASE STUDY: MOVING TO A NEW CITY

My friend Bri is a military wife and moves with her husband, Jeremy, and their dog every three years. That's a lot of moving, and moving is stressful for most people. How can Bri Lazy Genius moving to a new city? Let's run through the thirteen principles and find out.

Decide Once

What can Bri decide one time? She can have the same pattern for every move: week one is hard-core unpacking, week two is nesting, and week three is exploring. Always, in every city. That way she can focus on what matters right away (getting settled) and leave space for what will matter later (making the new city home).

Start Small

Moving to a new city is a huge undertaking, so it's easy to get caught up in the big stuff. Rather than looking at the mountains of boxes and being frozen by the enormity of the task, Bri and her husband can start with one box. One room. One hour at a time.

Ask the Magic Question

Before moving, what can Bri do to make things easier later? She can

- label the boxes really well so that unpacking is easier
- think through their go-to comfort recipes and separately pack the kitchen equipment they'll need to get started
- research the closest grocery store, coffee shop, and bagel place before all the unpacking craziness takes over and nobody wants to make a decision about anything else

Live in the Season

If anyone understands the value of living in the season, it's folks in the military.

Bri is allowed to feel sad about not having roots in one particular place for decades, but she can also embrace a different kind of rooting in this season. Her husband is doing something he's passionate about, she's a gamer and up for anything, and this season can be full of adventure and connection.

By choosing to live in her season and not despairing about what she's missing, Bri can embrace gratitude for the uniqueness of what she has.

Build the Right Routines

It's hard to live in a new place, and when the discouragement kicks in, it's easy to stay home and forget that the new city is waiting out there.

Still, Bri knows that learning this new city and making it home matters to her, so she can build a routine that leads her into a place of exploration and openness rather than one of isolation.

Perhaps she starts a simple morning routine of walking down the street to the local coffee place instead of making coffee herself. That simple act gets her out of the house and into her new city, and it helps her remember the joy of discovering what's around the corner.

Maybe she also feels overwhelmed by the smattering of boxes still needing to be unpacked, so she builds a simple routine of putting one thing away every time she enters a room. It's a small but effective routine that can easily be built upon when there's time to tackle more.

Set House Rules

Bri notices that her discouragement flares up when she goes several days without talking to anyone but Jeremy. She needs interaction with the human race, please! Yet it's hard to muster the courage to find it in a new city, especially when it feels like there's still so much to do.

Enter a new house rule: Bri will not go two days in a row without (safely) telling a stranger that she's new in the area and would love a recommendation for coffee or Thai food.

It's unlikely that the stranger will become a lifelong friend, but it is likely that Bri will feel connected to someone and feel the lightness this simple interaction offers her. Now she has a rule to not go two days in a row without seeking it out.

Put Everything in Its Place

The beauty of moving to a new city and a new home is that you have the chance to start over in giving everything a place. The problem with moving to a new city and a new home is that nothing has a place yet and you have to find a place for literally everything. Still, there's a gift in being able to intentionally do it.

Bri might be tempted to cram all their belongings into drawers and cabinets and take care of it later, but she'd regret that in no time. Even though it takes longer and might feel a little annoying, the Lazy Genius Way for Bri to move into a new home is to take the time to put everything in its place. She'll reap the rewards sooner than she might expect.

Let People In

This one is tough in a new city. How do you let people in when you don't know anyone?

First, Bri can let friends from past seasons of life into her loneliness. She doesn't have to keep it to herself and can share the struggle.

Second, she can take the tiny risk of going first and inviting someone new over for dinner. Maybe it's a neighbor, someone she meets at church or at CrossFit, or even a woman in line who orders the same coffee Bri does.

This might be the hardest principle when moving to a new place, but that's because it's one of the most crucial. For a place to feel like home, you have to let people in.

Bri can start small by going first.

Batch It

Unpacking is a great master class in batching. Unpack one entire box and batch where things should go rather than pulling out one thing, putting it away, and doing it over and over again.

Essentialize

It's likely Bri essentialized before she left her last home by putting energy into packing only what really matters. Moving is an excellent catalyst for naming what matters and keeping only what's essential to supporting it.

Go in the Right Order

Remember, the right order always starts with what matters, moves on to calming the crazy, and ends with trusting yourself.

For Bri and her husband, engaging with their neighbors and feeling at home both matter deeply.

How can they calm the crazy of what that entails? Craziness in this case might come from wondering if they're going to pick the right house in the right neighborhood. *What if we choose wrong? What if we pick a house but then wish we had picked a different neighborhood?*

They calm that crazy by living in Airbnbs in their favorite neighborhoods for the first few weeks in the new city. That might sound like the opposite of calming the crazy, but if the neighborhood matters that much, they can eliminate future crazy by naming what matters and trusting that this way of approaching where to live works for them.*

---

*Bri is a real person, by the way, and she actually does this. I'm still not over how brilliant it is.

Schedule Rest

This is a big one when moving to a new place.

Bri is both physically tired from traveling and unpacking and emotionally tired from the stress of all this change.

Rest is key. She can schedule one day a week to take a break from checking anything off her list, no matter how long it is. She and her husband can take a couple of nights a week to leave the unpacked boxes for a walk around downtown with their dog, with no agenda other than being together.

By not letting rest fall through the cracks, Bri embraces what matters (sanity comes to mind) and gets even more done later because she's fully rested and restored.

Be Kind to Yourself

And here's where Bri's Lazy Genius Way will shine.

There's a lot of pressure during a move. There's possibly hidden pressure on how quickly she'll make friends, how much her home will reflect her personality, and how easily she and her husband will handle the transition.

And it likely won't always go the way she hopes. She may feel lonely or frustrated or a little resentful that this is her way of life.

That's when she can be kind to herself. Bri can value who she is and where she is right now. She can mark moments of chatting with a neighbor by the mailbox or finding her way to the grocery store without needing GPS. She can celebrate with her husband at the end of every week in their new home, clinking glasses to living this adventure together.

Kindness toward herself will help her be kinder to everyone else.

LIVING LIKE A LAZY GENIUS

What I've laid out isn't an intricate system with dozens of moving parts. Half of these principles affect Bri's mind-set more than her tangible choices.

Still, when I read through these possibilities, I see this move to a new city as an authentic adventure. There are plenty of challenges and frustrations and first steps that could feel overwhelming, but by approaching the process through the lens of these Lazy Genius principles, Bri's move to a new city is colored with what matters to her, not with how she thinks she *should* be doing.

Don't build a big system.

Simply run your situation through these principles and see what comes to the surface.

QUICK CASE STUDY: LEARNING TO COOK

Maybe you want to take up a new activity, such as cooking, but it seems like too much just thinking about it. Rather than quitting before you start, employ Lazy Genius principles from the beginning.

Decide Once

Make the same six recipes until you feel confident in them.

Start Small

Don't be embarrassed about starting with the basics of, say, cooking pasta.

Ask the Magic Question

Meal prep in the morning so you're not rushed in the evening and can focus on the process.

Live in the Season

Lean into your little kids being underfoot. Also, go for summer burgers and winter stews.

Build the Right Routines

Every morning while you're making coffee, remind yourself what you planned for dinner.

Set House Rules

Always wear an apron when you cook to give yourself a sense of purpose.

Put Everything in Its Place

Create easy access to your kitchen tools so you're not scrambling as you try to learn a recipe.

Let People In

Invite someone over even though you don't think the food is good enough. That's not what matters.

Batch It

If chopping vegetables is your biggest frustration, do it all at once on a Sunday so you won't have to think about it the rest of the week.

Essentialize

Don't buy seventeen new pans. You need only one or two that will serve you well.

Go in the Right Order

What matters is calm confidence in the kitchen. Calm the crazy by releasing some of your standards and trust yourself.

Schedule Rest

Don't cook every night. It's good to take a break.

Be Kind to Yourself

Learning a new skill is hard, and you can celebrate where you are without being distracted by where you're not yet.

SOME FINAL THOUGHTS

As we come to the end, I want to say two things.

First, never ever feel guilty about what matters to you. If eating out and enjoying your city and engaging with strangers and being the life of the party matter to you, don't you dare think that's not valid because it doesn't look the same as someone who would rather have people around her kitchen table and go to bed at nine. Everything matters because *we* all matter, and different things matter to each of us. Name what matters to *you*. If it matters, it counts.

Second, you are enough. You can stop trying to be the ideal, future you, carrying a load you were never meant to carry. Let go of the working, the listing, the striving—all the things you're doing to deserve the love of the people around you. You are enough.

• • •

Now let's go back to the beach.

Rather than picking up a shovel or a bucket, grab your beach chair. Walk slowly to the edge of the water, nestle the chair into the soft sand, and sit.

Be still.

Feel wave after slow wave gently settle you deeper into the sand, anchoring you exactly where you are. Don't coax the waves to come faster or the sand to pile higher around you. Rest in the silence. Receive the stillness. Experience the beauty of your smallness.

One of my favorite things about being at the beach is how loud and silent it is at the same time. It's weird, right? The wind and waves are so loud that they muffle the voices and laughter around you, yet the sounds of the beach are among the most calming I know. It's a gentle ferocity.

When we quiet ourselves and experience stillness, the voice of God that was always there is easier to hear. We confidently sit where he has us and allow his presence to draw us deeper into where we are.

No digging, no buckets, no looking around at what everyone else is doing. We simply receive and respond to the

> **We become a generation of women who are at peace with who we are, who encourage one another to move closer to our deepest identities and shed what's in the way.**

power of our precious, powerful Father. And the longer we sit and the deeper we sink, the more excited we are to invite other tired friends to pull up their beach chairs and join us.

And imagine this. We become a generation of women who are at peace with who we are, who encourage one another to move closer to our deepest identities and shed what's in the way. I'm all for that world.

Stop trying so hard, friend.

Stop trying to build it big.

You weren't knit together in your mother's womb so you could run after a moving finish line. You're tired because you're trying to overcome the world, but we can take heart because the God of the universe has already done that.

You are fearfully and wonderfully made.

He has hemmed you in behind and before.

His thoughts for you are impossible to count.

That's not a God who gets a laugh watching you drown in the deep end of life as you try to manage schedules and chores and ridiculous expectations. The indwelling Christ is with you, and you can just *be*.

Hear this now, friend: You are loved. You are seen. You are enough.

With tears in my eyes, I thank you. It's been one of the deepest honors of my life to enter your life with these words.

I'm rooting for you.

ACKNOWLEDGMENTS

When I thought about writing a book, I figured this would be the easy part. Turns out, coming up with sufficient words to thank all the people who have been with me through this whole "let's write a book" thing is incredibly difficult. There simply aren't enough words said in the right way to communicate how thankful I am for these people.

First, thank you, beautiful Lazy Genius community. This book is for you and wouldn't exist without you. Thank you for listening to podcast episodes, making Change-Your-Life Chicken, and cheering me on in ways more valuable than you can possibly know. I'm grateful for your kindness, your questions, and your ability to know the perfect James McAvoy GIF to put in an Instagram DM. You are amazing, and I wish I could bake you all cookies.

A massive thank you to my team at WaterBrook: Susan Tjaden for making my words better, Johanna Inwood for caring about the character of marketing more than the numbers, Lisa Beech and Chelsea Woodward for working so hard to get this message out there, and all the other folks I never met who nonetheless worked so hard to make this book come to life. Thank you, thank you, thank you.

Lisa Jackson, you have been such an advocate for me. Thank you for suffering through my rambling Voxer messages, for believing in me when I thought I'd made a huge mistake, and for being not just my agent but also my friend.

Leah Jarvis, you are the wind beneath my wings. Thank you for quitting your job to work for me, for knowing my brain better than I sometimes do, and for being an all-around delightful human. I'm so honored to have you in my corner.

Emily P. Freeman, I truly don't know how to do things without you. Thank you for naming what I can't name and seeing what I can't see, from parenting to writing and everything in between. You have been my door to Oz—to this colorful, weird world of sharing my words that has made me more myself than I knew was possible. The work I do, the person I've become, the dreams I've put into the world would not exist without you. You're such a gift, and I love you.

Jamie B. Golden, what would've happened if I'd never emailed you to pitch myself as your friend? Oh, how sad my world would be without you in it. You've been a surprise, my friend, teaching me the value of celebration and the gift of possibility. You're also the funniest person I know, and I'm a better human because you're my friend.

Bri McKoy and Laura Tremaine, who along with Jamie have been the mastermind group of my dreams, thank you for listening to me say far too many words about very unimportant things, for helping me solve my business problems, and for sending me screenshots of the iTunes ranking of my podcast in pure celebration. You ladies are the absolute best, and I love you so much.

Myquillyn Smith, Caroline Teselle, Tsh Oxenreider, and Emily P. Freeman, thank you for being a safe place to feel like a professional idiot. Your collective wisdom over the years has been so amazing it's almost stupid. I'm so grateful for the hours and weekends and conversations from North Carolina to London that have shaped my work and life. I'm so honored to call you friends.

Erin Moon, you're the coolest chick on the internet and the greatest muse I could ask for. You've brought me more clarity in my work and joy in my life than you probably know. I'm so glad the internet brought us together.

Knox McCoy, you're a killer editor, and your encouragement in this process has been such a gift. Thanks for being so good at what you do, for giving me thoughtful insight on these words, and for being a super nice guy to boot.

Anne Bogel, your timing in checking in on me through this process was eerie and amazing. Thank you for being such a faithful encouragement to me.

To all the musicians who were my constant companions during this process: Penny & Sparrow, Songs of Water, Slow Meadow, the Gloaming, Yasmin Williams, Ólafur Arnalds, and Balmorhea. You have my deepest gratitude. I'm not myself without music, so thanks for helping me feel whole when things got squirrely.

To my precious, ridiculously amazing church family and community group at Hope Chapel: your friendships couldn't have come at a better time, and I'm consistently bowled over at how great I have it here with you. Love you for real.

Elizabeth and Charlie Swing, Andraya and Daniel Northrup, and Griffin and Erin Kale, thank you for cheering me on in ways I never expected. You are beautiful friends.

Jason and Alisa Windsor, I will always remember this book as the project I was working on when you got the call that

Alistair was yours. What a gift to have you as friends, to know how much you both believe in my work and how long you have been rooting for it, and to live life together through these last few upside-down years. I love you both, and praise Jesus for that sweet baby in your arms.

Hannah Van Patter, thank you for the notes on my desk, the cake on my birthday, the family dinners on deadline days, and your kind, steadfast friendship. You're such a gift, and I'm beyond grateful for how well you have loved me. Michael, cheers to all the nerding out over pizza, and thanks for building me that wall. Our family loves yours so very much, and we can't wait to keep doing life together. Thank you for going first.

Mom and Jon, thank you for being such supportive parents, for faithfully praying for me through this process, and for being proud of me for no other reason than because I'm me. I love you both.

Tom and Seiko, thank you for feeding Kaz and the kids so often while I was working and for cheering on my dreams. You are wonderful in-laws, and I'm grateful for you.

To Luke, Hannah, Imi, Silas, Miles, Matt, Julie, Morgan, Ava, Kennedy, Emmaline, Jeremiah, Chris, Becky, Ivy, Tet, Kenji, Christine, Charis, Alana, and Derek: what a gift to have you all as family.

Hannah Kody, thank you for knowing my stories better than I do, for helping me figure out my hair, for laughing at jokes no one else understands, for knowing the underbelly of who I am and loving me even more because of it. Simply put, you are the best. I love you like a sister (because you are), but I'm so glad you're my friend.

Sam, Ben, and Annie, y'all are without a doubt the coolest,

kindest kids around. I love you so much my heart could explode, and being your mom is an honor.

Kaz, I'd pick you again and again and again. Your love made me come alive and is my safest place to land. I love you, and the last one listed in my acknowledgments is a rotten egg.

NOTES

1. James Clear, *Atomic Habits* (New York: Avery, 2018), 21.
2. Gary Keller and Jay Papasan, *The ONE Thing* (Austin, TX: Bard Press, 2013), 113.
3. Brené Brown, *The Gifts of Imperfection* (Center City, MN: Hazelden, 2010), 26.
4. Myquillyn Smith, *The Nesting Place* (Grand Rapids, MI: Zondervan, 2014), 61.
5. Greg McKeown, *Essentialism* (New York: Crown Business, 2014), 55.
6. Emily P. Freeman, "Sit Down on the Inside," episode 62, *The Next Right Thing,* podcast, 16:39, https://emilypfreeman .com/podcast/the-next-right-thing/62.
7. Clear, *Atomic Habits,* 24.

ABOUT THE AUTHOR

KENDRA ADACHI went to college to become a high school English teacher but instead became the Lazy Genius, passionately and candidly sharing how to stop doing it all for the sake of doing what matters. Her work includes hosting *The Lazy Genius Podcast*, cooking dinner on Instagram, and convincing her three young kids that talking into the phone is Mommy's job. She and her husband love raising their family in the same North Carolina city where they both grew up.

Yes, We Do Need Another Time Management Book

I have a long history of being meticulous.

As a kid, I enjoyed folding laundry into beautiful piles, vacuuming to get those breathtaking carpet lines, and shelving my Nancy Drew books by publication date. I knew how to make my bed with hospital corners as a third grader *because I asked my mom to show me how.*

As a teenager, I got even cooler. I had an impeccable work ethic, a perpetually clean room, and a stack of notebooks that held my future goals, my favorite movies, and, inexplicably, my classmates' names in alphabetical order. By first *and* last name. I still don't understand why.

You might think that as a grown woman I would've relaxed a little, but you would be wrong. I had a color-coded binder of every helpful *Real Simple* article ever published, an annual cleaning schedule on my fridge (yes, I said *annual*), and enough five-year plans to fill a dozen lifetimes. And please don't ask me to count how many planners I've purchased in my twentyish years of adulthood. The answer is likely in the triple digits, and our relationship needs more time before I'm that vulnerable.

In short, I love it when my life is in order.

However, in my early thirties, after bringing three kids and two side hustles into the world, I was bone tired from just living my life, and I could not figure out why. I had done the right things! I had read dozens of the most popular self-help books and organized my life according to their principles, but all that did was make me a caffeinated squirrel on a treadmill.

I thought the problem was me. Maybe I didn't have enough discipline or consistency. Maybe I had misidentified my goals and therefore couldn't make them happen. Maybe I needed a new *planner.*

Bless.

Because I consistently experienced a disconnect between popular self-help strategies and my actual life, I felt I needed to bridge the gap, but I couldn't figure out how.

That's why I wrote my first book, *The Lazy Genius Way.* It's a collection of thirteen principles that you can apply to any problem in any season of life.* It's a personal, versatile approach to living a good life based on what matters to you, instead of choosing a life because someone else said it was good. In fact, *The Lazy Genius Way* felt so comprehensive to me that I thought it would be my only book.

Again, bless.

My second book, *The Lazy Genius Kitchen,* applied those same thirteen Lazy Genius principles to the kitchen, and right after its release, I was confident that was my last book. What else could I possibly say?

This, apparently.

The initial idea for *The PLAN* did not come from anything interesting, like a lightbulb moment in the shower or an idea written on a cocktail napkin in the darkened bowels of a dive bar. Nope. It came from data analysis. Riveting.

I run a content-creation business, and it's important for my

---

*You can find them in the Quick-Reference Guide at the end of the book.

team and me to know what content resonates so we can know what to create. The data says that the most popular episodes of *The Lazy Genius Podcast* are, by a significant margin, all related to time management. Annual survey responses say the same: "Kendra, you can stop talking about the other stuff; just talk to us about how to not drown in our to-do lists!"

And frankly, I'm good at it. At my core, I'm still the third grader who loves hospital corners and alphabetized lists, but I'm also an adult who's had enough therapy, failure, and rewarding relationships to put my love of order in a healthy context. As a result, I enjoy speaking about refreshing and occasionally subversive ways to manage our time so we can just *live our lives.*

But as I flirted with what this book could be, I noticed something that changed everything—I am a woman.

I mean, I knew that already, but in the context of time management books? There aren't a lot of us. In fact, 93 percent of time management books are written by men. Ninety-actual-three.*

Guess what that means?

The problem isn't you.

It's not your lack of dedication, consistency, or motivation. It's not because you haven't started the right habit or taken the right online course. It's because the current productivity paradigm doesn't work for women. It's that simple. The advice you're getting is for men by men, and women are just expected to make it work.

Think about it. Most time-management authors and experts are men who do not have a boss, a home to run, or a menstrual

---

*I did my own analysis of the top selling books over several decades, recommended reading lists, and what is on store shelves. Whether the sample size was seventeen or seventeen hundred, the number written by men was always 93 percent. Wild.

cycle. I don't know if you're aware, but all three are notoriously unwieldy. And if you're not wielding them on a regular basis, it's much easier to create your ideal life.

The current productivity paradigm doesn't work for women.

If you don't have a boss, you can craft a work schedule where you check email twice a day and go home at 3 p.m. If you're not managing meals, moods, and the entire family calendar, you can prioritize your health, friendships, and leisure. If you're unaffected by weekly hormonal fluctuations, you can create an ideal day and replicate it.

In general, a man's life is oriented around *him,* and a woman's life is oriented around everything *but her,* all while her body's rhythms are annoyingly inconvenient.

This exclusion is why most productivity books are incomplete. They were written by and for a certain subset, and you are likely not in that subset. You will struggle to follow their rules because you're not meant to play their game.

Of course, there's nothing wrong with a man's system and the authors who keep it standing. I'm glad they have approaches that work for their particular lives, but they don't comprehensively work for ours. The current productivity landscape misses us—women and anyone else who lives outside the traditional white-male experience—and I'm tired of so many people being missed.

For the record, this book is not anti–white guy. I love white guys. (I'd say I'm married to one, but that would be a lie since my husband, Kaz, is Japanese.) Some of my favorite books are written by white guys. Some of my favorite friends are white guys. I'm not knocking them in general or in the context of productivity.

I simply want to acknowledge that the current time-management paradigm is *not for us.* The loudest voices are not our voices, and their strategies are not what we need.

And that is why we *do* need another time-management book.

How to Read This Book

I've divided *The PLAN* into three sections: principles, strategies, and pep talks. I tried to make them all start with a *p,* but it was a lost cause.

Part 1 teaches the **principles** of *The PLAN.* Since belief comes before behavior, you need to understand *why* before you learn *how.*

Part 2 is that *how.* In it, I'll teach you **strategies** for managing your time that are practical, tangible, and without an ounce of bootstrap energy.

Part 3 is an entire section of **pep talks.** Each one is specific to a particular time-management struggle, and they are not meant to be read all at once. Instead, when you feel off-kilter, skim the pep talk titles, read one that resonates, and then get back to your life with your feet a little firmer on the ground.

The PLAN is full of lists, steps, and frameworks (all drenched in humanity and compassion, I promise), and you might want to remember something without skimming the entire book to find it. In those instances, go straight to the Quick-Reference Guide.

The PLAN is intended to be your time management companion from this day forward. Write in it. Dog-ear pages. Use one highlighter color for your personal life and another color for your work life. Keep *The PLAN* with your planner. Regularly read a pep talk. Revisit the principles when you feel overwhelmed by your life. Try a new strategy during a new season.

Every reading will illuminate something new.

I'm grateful to be here with you, honored by your trust, and hopeful you will reach for this book often.

Let's get started.